MARY KING

MY WAY
How I train for success

Edited by Jane Gazzard and Aimi Clark

MARY KING

A CIP catalogue record for this book is available from The British Library.

HARDBACK ISBN 978-0-9929951-0-2

Printed in Great Britain by Acanthus Press, Wellington, Somerset TA21 9PZ

Editors Jane Gazzard, Deputy Editor of Horse&Rider magazine
Aimi Clark is a content producer with Horse&Hound and Eventing magazines

Designer Paul Smail, Designer with PONY Magazine

Photography Front cover: Iain Burns
Back cover: Bob Atkins
Inside: Bob Atkins, with additional photography by Iain Burns, Natalie Clark, Hugo M Czerny, Mandy Davis/Equine Sports Photography, Equestrian Services Thorney, Barry Gomer, Trevor Holt, Liz Knowler, Trevor Meeks, J-B de Monléon

Mary with Call Again Cavalier (left)
and Imperial Cavalier

Foreword

Being a successful event rider is not just about being a good competitor and having a winner's instinct – it is about selecting the right horse, educating and training it, and preparing the horse and yourself. Mary has shown over a long and illustrious career that she is very knowledgeable in all of these aspects. Her success has been based on not just what she does at the competitions, but also what is done in her yard and her training, day in and day out.

As Performance Manager for the British Event Team, I have had the privilege and the opportunity to get an in-depth insight of Mary, not just as a competitive rider but also as a horsewoman. She has developed a very thorough system in how she educates and develops her horses from when they are young, unruly, boisterous, potential superstars right through to when they fulfil their true potential – and many of them have become household names. Mary has also shown a remarkable ability to keep her horses at the top for a long period of time, and many of them have competed well into their teens. This has only been possible due to her knowledge and experience, and the very thorough system that she has developed over many years.

It is great that Mary has taken time out to write this book where, in a simple and easy way to understand, she shares the philosophies behind her well tried and successful system. She is sharing with all of us her in-depth knowledge and great experience. In this book, there is something for everyone, whether you are a young aspiring event rider or have already achieved success, whether you just enjoy the sport as a pastime or you are a professional. I am sure the knowledge that you will gain from Mary's book will stand you in good stead in your eventing career.

The one thing that has stood out in Mary's career has been that she has never stopped learning, and this book gives us all the opportunity to continue to learn from a master.

Yogi Breisner
Performance Manager, Eventing and Lead for World Class Programme Coach & Staff Development

Contents

Welcome to 'Mary King — My Way'

I love my horses and I love the sport of eventing. However, the euphoria of passing through the cross-country finish flags is the result of a lot of hard work and dedication. I believe that the key to being a successful rider is having a good everyday routine in place. It doesn't matter if you're a professional event rider or competing as a hobby, solid foundations will set you up to achieve the best from yourself and your horse. You must be prepared to keep learning and improving – I still am!

This book is about 'my way'. It reveals how I run my yard and how I train and care for my horses. There may be parts that would not suit other yards, but it works for mine and I am always confident that my horses are happy, healthy and ready to perform.

'My way' is built on years of advice from trainers, other riders and learning from experiences throughout my 30-year career. My daughter, Emily, appears in many of the pictures as we train alongside each other and, for the first time, we have opened the doors to our world in order to share the secrets of success for competing at grassroots level and beyond. I hope that it will be a catalyst in helping you achieve your dreams.

Good luck with your horses . . .

Mary King

My horses
The horses who feature in the following pages

Imperial Cavalier ('Archie') is owned by Edwin and Sue Davies, and Janette Chinn. He had seven top six placings at CCI**** level and was part of the gold medal-winning team at the 2010 World Championships, silver medal team at the 2012 Olympics and bronze medal team at the 2011 European Championships. Archie retired this year at the age of 17.

Kings Choice ('Lottie') is a six-year-old mare by Cavalier Royale, owned by Peter Appleford, John Bevan and Roger and Jill Trivett. Lottie upgraded to Intermediate level after winning the Novice at Chatsworth in May 2014.

King Dan ('Dan') is five years old and a new ride for me this season. He is competing at BE100 level.

Miss Indigo ('Indie') is Emily's ride. Owned by Patsy Mason, Indie is seven and competing at Intermediate level, and completed her first CIC** in 2014.

Del Piero II ('Peter') belongs to a long-term owner of mine, Gillian Jonas. Peter was bought for Emily, who has produced him up to Intermediate level, winning the ONu18 at Chatsworth in May 2014.

And not forgetting my dog, Barney, who can be spotted in many of the pictures. He is very good with the horses and he loves going hacking or for trips in the lorry. Barney is a two-year-old brown and white collie and I have had him since he was a puppy – he is a member of the family.

Distances and jumps explained

When I am building fences at home and walking courses at an event, I work with the following distances...

- **Trotting poles**
  1 step between every pole

- **Canter poles**
  3 steps between every pole

- **1 stride**
  8 steps (2 for the landing,
  4 for 1 stride, 2 for take-off)

- **2 strides**
  12 steps (2 for the landing, 4 for the first stride, 4 for the second stride,
  2 for take-off)

- **3 strides**
  16 steps (2 for the landing, 4 for the first stride, 4 for the second stride,
  4 for the third stride, 2 for take-off)

- **Bounce**
  3½ steps between two fences

These distances are approximate as it depends on the size of your horse's stride. For example, each step is roughly 1 metre, but tall horses will naturally cover more ground with each stride than ponies.

The showjumps I refer to in this book are...

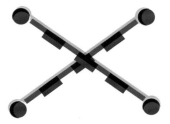

Cross-pole
Two poles crossing each other to form an X shape, clearly showing where the centre of the fence is

Ground pole
Ground poles are useful in training as they make the ground line and, therefore, the take-off point clear for horses to see

Upright/vertical
A rail running straight across from one wing to the other. This requires a ground pole

Spread/oxer
Two rails running straight between the wings, one pole in front of the other. The front pole can be slightly lower or at the same height as the pole behind.

MANAGEMENT

An organised, workable routine will keep your horse happy and focused

Choose a horse
who is naturally
athletic

What makes an event horse?

- **Natural athleticism** ● **Why good paces are important**
- **The natural galloper** ● **Temperament is key**

The aim

Generally speaking, if you want to have a fighting chance of succeeding at the level you event at, choose a horse who is naturally athletic and who moves well, especially if you're aiming for the higher levels. It's natural athleticism that makes a horse light on his feet and that, together with good limb conformation, means he'll have a better chance of standing up to what's being asked of him.

Bear in mind, you can't make an unathletic horse a super athlete – it's impossible to completely change this dimension of his make-up. But the more naturally athletic he is, the more he should be able to cope with slight conformational defects.

I like a horse to be naturally light on his feet, because the more naturally athletic a horse is, the longer he's going to last – and that's important if you are aiming to progress to Advanced level.

Paces

An event horse must have three good paces. The further you want to climb up the levels, the more impressive the movement and natural look of the horse has to be. Having said that, however, even being placed at the lower levels of affiliated competition still requires a very good dressage test, so three good paces are important.

Walk

The horse needs to be purposeful in his walk and naturally overtrack – that is, where the hind feet step in front of the hoofprints left by the front feet.

Three good paces are important

Trot

The same applies to the trot. The horse must have a purposeful way of going with a good length of stride, one that is not flat, but showing some roundness and elevation.

Canter

If the horse canters naturally in a balanced way – that is, with his hindleg coming well underneath his body – he'll find his work easier. However, it can also mean that he does not have such a good gallop, so there's a very fine line to be drawn here.

A Thoroughbred, which is bred for speed, doesn't step under with his hindlegs as naturally as most warmbloods. He uses his long hindlegs to propel himself forward.

The more naturally he gallops, the easier the fast work

The gallop

It goes without saying that an event horse must gallop well. I've had horses who I've thought would be quick enough, but when I've taken them up a gear, they've struggled. Bear in mind that the more naturally a horse can gallop, the easier he'll find the fast work and the less he will struggle as far as fitness and stamina are concerned – therefore, the less chance of sustaining an injury.

needs to jump – you want to put your time and effort into a horse who is capable of jumping reasonably well. Generally, though, success depends a lot on the horse's attitude, so bear in mind that the easier he finds the work, the more he'll enjoy it.

As far as the actual mechanics of jumping are concerned, the quicker a horse is in front – as in the quicker he is in snapping up his front legs off the ground and folding them away over a jump – the better. Horses like this are less likely to leave a leg at a fence and as a result, you'll be less likely to take a tumble.

A good horse should also be relatively careful with his hindlegs, but he doesn't need to make the amazing bascule (the natural round arc a horse's body makes over a jump) that pure showjumpers do. In fact, there are some event horses who jump in quite peculiar shapes, but are still very efficient. So as long as your horse can clear the fence comfortably, that's what you should be considering.

A good horse should be careful with their hindlegs

Anyone for walkies?

The jump

Their natural jump is one of the most important requirements of an event horse. Horses are just like people – some can run along and jump over something very easily while others can't, and horses are the same. However, depending on how competitive you are determines how well the horse

Temperament

At the end of the day, the event horse's temperament is paramount. You can have a horse with all the talent in the world, but if he can't cope mentally with the training and competing – including coping with playful dogs like Barney, above – he will never fulfil his potential.

Buying an event horse

- **Conformation** ● **My horses**
- **No foot, no horse** ● **Strengths and weaknesses**

I like a good-looking horse

Whether beginning at riding club level, progressing through the lower levels of affiliated competition towards Novice or competing at the top end at Advanced level, we all hope to find the horse of our dreams, the best horse for our budget and one who can do the job for us.

There are, however, many things to consider when buying a horse to event, and depending on how competitive you are as a person has quite a bearing on the sort of horse you should be looking for. But as a general rule, the main point that needs to be considered, no matter what level you ride at, is conformation.

A big eye is thought to mean kindness – as in the case of Imperial Cavalier

Body

Look for a horse who is correctly put together, with the neck set high on a good sloping shoulder – this will give him more chance of moving well and of being a good galloper. A low-set neck on the other hand – ie, the horse built on the forehand with a lower head carriage – means that he'll probably find it much more difficult to produce the self-carriage required for the dressage phase. A low-set neck can put a horse more on the forehand for the jumping phases – and it can also mean he is more likely to overload onto his front legs so there's more chance of injury.

I look for a horse who's not too long or too short in the back and with a nicely rounded bottom – although with a young horse, his hindquarters might not be that well-developed. Even so, I like a youngster to carry his tail straight when working, especially at trot and canter – if it's held tight down or to one side, it could indicate that there's something wrong with his back.

Head

For me personally, a good head is important because I do admittedly like good-looking horses such as Imperial Cavalier (aka Archie). An intelligent, kind eye is attractive too, and a nice, big eye is thought to mean the horse is kind – certainly the case with Archie. It's also thought that a horse with big ears is more genuine.

Ideally, in the throat area – between the two round jawbones – there should be a good width into which you can fit a fist, meaning that the head is nicely broad with a flat forehead.

Limbs

Obviously, keeping an event horse sound is vital, so he can't afford to have too many conformational problems. He must have a reasonable amount of bone even if he is a quality Thoroughbred, but not be overly long in the cannon bones. And a strong, active hindleg is important, because if a horse is lazy in the hindleg, he'll always be lazy in the hindleg – and that's difficult to activate. So he'll find engagement and collection more difficult.

A correct hoof pastern axis

Feet

An event horse must have strong feet, especially if you're aiming to compete at the higher levels. There should be a natural angle with the foot and pastern – called the hoof pastern axis – the norm being about 45 degrees.

When it comes to the feet, bear in mind the old adage, 'No foot, no horse' so steer clear of a horse who is flat-footed with shallow heels or one who has 'boxy' front feet with high heels. On either count, soundness could become a problem, creating more chance of bruised soles and corns. And boxy feet can cause concussion issues, therefore more stress up through the leg.

My horse

When it comes to good conformation for an event horse, King William was an exception to the rule. He had quite poor lower limb conformation and I remember being very concerned, even embarrassed, when I decided to go ahead and have him vetted before buying him, because I knew what the vet would say – that I was mad! However, I just loved the way he moved – he was naturally athletic and light on his feet, and he carried himself well. But he had pigeon toes, he was slightly tied in below the knee – meaning he lacked bone directly below the knee – and he had false curbs on both hind hocks. He was, however, one of the soundest horses I've ever had.

King William didn't have the greatest shaped hooves either, but I have a very good farrier – Nick Rule – and I've learnt over the years that it is only worth getting the best to shoe your horse. If your farrier has to travel slightly further, at the end of the day he can probably help make savings on those vets' bills and hopefully promote the longevity of your horse's career.

King William

Kings Choice – smaller but still with enormous potential

Height

Although I personally prefer a bigger horse (Imperial Cavalier was 17hh), I do have smaller horses on my yard who I enjoy riding as well, such as Kings Choice (aka Lottie, above, who's 16.1hh). However, I always find that the bigger the horse, the smaller the fences look!

When deciding on the height of a new horse, simply go with what you're comfortable with. As a rider, you know what your weaknesses are – for example, if you're not such a good jumping or dressage rider, try to choose a horse who will help you with your weaker areas. Equally, your horse's weaknesses may be your strengths, and something that you can help him with. When all's said and done, it's all about teamwork and it's often how you feel on the day when you see the horse as to whether you buy him.

For best results

- In your search for the perfect event horse, temperament is probably the most important ingredient. So look for a trainable, genuine, happy horse with whom you can build a successful lasting partnership – he'll be worth his weight in gold!

Feed a balanced diet

The aim

Ever since I started riding, I've been a great believer in attention to detail and I soon learnt that success begins with the small, incidental things. I believe that if horses live in an organised environment, then the better prepared they'll be for competing.

Having a workable routine in place helps reduce the risk of injuries, setbacks and silly mistakes, because as soon as you start cutting corners, that's when things go wrong.

My way

In the mornings, we hang up the haylage nets so that mucking out is easier. Once we've finished mucking out, we empty the haylage onto the floor so that the horses can eat with their heads down – it replicates the way they naturally eat in the field. But the evening haylage nets are emptied onto the floor immediately.

My daily routine

- **A typical day** ● **The best bedding**
- **Turnout and grooming** ● **Regular checks**

7am

Emily or I feed the horses, washing out the feed buckets thoroughly and letting them drain afterwards. We'll also straighten rugs and check legs – it's important to know what is normal for each horse so that we can spot any potential problem immediately. I'll check on the mares and youngstock living out in a field in the valley and run my hands over the youngsters' bodies so they get used to me touching them. This promotes a developing connection between horse and human, so the trust starts to build.

7.30am

My girl grooms – Lauren Reed and Emma Hartwell – muck out, taking 20 minutes a stable. I'm quite fussy about the horse's bedding, so I use Nedz Bed Pro which is made from chopped oil seed rape straw. What I like about it is that it is virtually dust-free and that helps eradicate the harmful mould spores that can lead to respiratory problems in the horse – which is obviously something we try to avoid. Another great plus-point is that because it's highly absorbent, it soaks up the urine that can

Mucking out takes 20 minutes a stable

lead to high levels of ammonia, which can damage the hoof and cause thrush – again, something else we try to avoid, bearing in mind that the competition horses are stabled for long

periods of time. But then the Nedz Bed products do contain an organic treatment that provides antiseptic and anti-bacterial properties that help keep the stables hygienic. What's more, Nedz Bed rots down nicely and can be used as an effective natural fertiliser.

All stables are fitted with a single layer of StableComfort Superior rubber flooring, a product I've used for over 10 years now. Rubber chip-filled mattresses are laid on the concrete base, with a latex-coated top cover that is fixed to the walls and continues right to the door of the stable, so that no dust or dirt gets trapped under the mattress. The top cover is also waterproof so no dampness seeps through to the under-mattress.

StableComfort provides a spongey comfortable bed

Once Lauren and Emma have mucked out, they'll empty, clean then refill the water buckets – two per stable – taking note of how much water the horses have drunk so that we know on average what their daily intake is. That way we can notice if there's a sudden change that could indicate the horse isn't feeling on top form.

Then Lauren and Emma will sweep up and tidy the muck trailer. The haylage nets are filled for the evening and the following morning. In all the stables, I've used some lovely, old-fashioned butler sinks as mangers and while I'm not suggesting they're to everyone's taste, they work well for me.

My flooring

StableComfort replicates natural pasture in terms of providing a more comfortable environment for your horse, at the same time reducing maintenance and bedding requirements, although I do like to put some bedding on top.

Stabled horses often spend lengthy periods of time on their feet, so the spongey, cushioned feel to this flooring – and the fact that its top cover is non-slip and there's plenty of 'give' in the under-mattress, unlike other common rubber matting which can be quite hard – provides a sure footing for them. This encourages them to lie down more often, mirroring their natural behaviour in pasture and, therefore, reducing stress and assisting in injury recovery.

The horses get worked through the morning – our normal weekly routine involves fast work every third day, with schooling, jumping and hacking in-between. Lauren and Emma help with hacking and some of the canter work, while Emily and I do all the schooling and jumping. After work, they're washed off if necessary, then turned out with rugs and exercise boots for a couple of hours.

We bring the horses in, groom them, then pick out and scrub the feet if necessary, hoof-oil inside and out, check the shoes and legs, then rug them up if necessary. Before lunch, we make sure all the stables are skipped out, beds are tidy and water buckets full. Any horse who's in has a lunchtime feed at 1pm and we'll leave feeds in the mangers of those who were worked late morning and were out over lunchtime. Then it's our lunchtime from 1-2pm.

Back in after two hours' turnout

2pm

Bring in the horses who were out over lunch. The afternoon is a good time for catching up with other random jobs – from cleaning mangers or stable windows, to giving the yard a thorough sweep. The lorry, too, has to be kept clean so it will be washed on the outside if it's just back from an event, then the next day it will be cleaned out completely so that it's ready for the next journey. Then there's a list of odd jobs pinned up in the tack

room that includes tack cleaning; poo-picking the fields in summer and sweeping the horse walker after each use; washing and pulling manes and tails, and trimming whiskers and ears.

We wash the feed bowls after each feed

4.30pm

The girls tidy the tack room, sweep the floor, and make sure the sink and surfaces are clean and mugs washed. Then the stables are skipped out, the beds tidied and the water buckets (two per stable) are topped up. Rugs are straightened then just before 5pm, the horses have their haylage – we empty the night haylage nets into a corner of the stable. Then after locking the tack room, it's home time for Lauren and Emma at 5pm.

6pm

Either Emily or I feed the horses and check their legs, but once the horses have had their last feed, that's it for the night and they won't see us again until morning. It's a routine that works well and I've never found a late-night check or feed to be necessary. But we do live on site so if there are any major problems, we're on hand to attend to them.

My way

When we turn out, I turn my horses out in twos or threes which shocks some people. However, I think it's worse risking injury to a lonely horse who is galloping up and down the field because he's missing his friends. We find that the horses get to know each other quite quickly as they get used to the routine, so that works well all round.

Remember!

It is important that you have a strict worming regime for your horse. I use Equest and Pramox, and worm every three months.

Feeding for performance

- **Stabled horses' menu** ● **Making dietary adjustments**
- **Feeding off the field** ● **The importance of forage**

The aim

When feeding any performance horse, it's important to ensure they receive a balanced diet. This enables their bodies to have the necessary nutrients to support performance, build muscle and make ongoing tissue repair, as well as the calories to fuel work while maintaining the right body condition. My horses have access to good grass through daily turnout and quality haylage, to provide digestible fibre – plus other nutrients as a correct basis for their diets.

Stabled horses

I feed Baileys Horse Feeds, and one of their nutritionists comes to assess the horses' feed plan, the first visit being when the horses come in from winter turnout to start work at the beginning of January. Their diet will be reassessed at the end of February when they're fitter and are doing faster work, then if I have any concerns during the season, I'll simply call Baileys for advice. My stabled horses have hard feed three times a day...

7am breakfast Haylage; Baileys Everyday High Fibre Cubes, Performance Balancer and Ultra Grass chaff. Chaff helps to bulk up the feed and encourage the horses to chew properly – the better doers get low-calorie Light Chaff, while those who need help maintaining condition get Ultra Grass.

1pm lunch High Fibre Cubes.

5pm tea Haylage.

6pm dinner The same as breakfast.

All my horses are turned out every day unless it's seriously wet. They'll be in the field for a good couple of hours, which is a chance for them to ingest some natural goodness.

My supplements

If a horse starts to look a bit 'tucked up' due to the excitement of travelling and competing, I'll feed Digest Plus prebiotic to help support a healthy gut and promote better digestive efficiency.

I'll also add a level teaspoonful of salt to my horses' evening feeds – usually from the second week of February once they've started their fast work and started to sweat more, as it's vital to replace valuable nutrients. Then as the weather heats up, I increase their salt intake – by the peak of the summer, they'll be having a level teaspoonful of salt in their morning and evening feeds. The stabled horses also have Rockies mineral licks to help themselves to whenever they feel they're lacking any minerals and salts.

Healthy eating

Food for thought

- **Any of my horses having a holiday or in light work** will receive sufficient calories from their forage (grass and haylage) alone, so don't need the extra provided by a mix or cube. These are fed just a balancer to provide quality protein, vitamins and minerals that are likely to be lacking in their forage, but without the calories associated with other concentrate feeds.

- **Horses who can be fizzy** are fed High Fibre Cubes then I top them up with balancer, while others may eat Baileys All-Round Endurance Mix. This is a high-oil, high-fibre competition mix that provides slow-release energy and helps promote stamina.

- **Horses in hard work and any who struggle to maintain condition** are fed Baileys Outshine, especially my older horses when they're getting fit and competing at a high level. It's a high-oil supplement and concentrated source of slow-release energy (calories) that can be added to an existing balanced diet. What's more, it makes their coats lovely and shiny!

Henny's always around at feed time

Feeding off the field

My five- and six-year-olds are out 24/7, and work and compete from the field. And while they do tend to churn up the fields in the winter, being out is much better for them mentally and physically as they keep moving around. I will, however, adjust their hard feed intake to take into account the extra calories provided by lush spring and summer grazing. Therefore, they'll have just a feed balancer each day, as well as the grazing to provide essential vitamins and minerals.

However, as the nutrients deplete when the grass dies off as winter approaches, they'll have extra feed – High Fibre Cubes with the balancer because the cubes alone do not contain sufficient vitamins, minerals and protein to be fed on their own to horses in work. Then when it gets colder, they'll also have haylage in the field. They have one hard feed a day in the morning, fed in bowls that slot inside tyres so that they're not knocked over. And they'll have the haylage in a pile secured under a hedge.

My young horses compete from the field

Forage

Whether you own a companion Shetland pony or a competition horse, the most important part of their feeding regime should be top-quality forage. As well as providing essential nutrients, the digestion of forage produces heat, so it's a vital tool to help keep your horse warm when the months turn colder.

I use Marksway HorseHage bagged haylage because the quality is consistent. It's available in four varieties with differing nutritional values so there's a choice to suit every type of horse or pony. There are three main types – Rygrass, High Fibre and Timothy – that contain just natural grass, with the High Fibre and Timothy varieties being suitable for laminitics, and there's also an Alfalfa variety.

I personally like the high-fibre variety because it's most similar to hay. This means that you can feed more during the day, which replicates the horses' little-and-often method of feeding out in the wild.

Forage is the most important ingredient

I find that HorseHage bagged forage offers many benefits compared to hay or ordinary haylage. For example, it's dust-free which is vital for maintaining a healthy respiratory tract and preventing conditions such as RAO (Recurrent Airway Obstruction). This is especially important when your horse has to be stabled for extended periods of time, as most of mine are, and essential for any horse or pony who is competing.

It also contains no chemical additives or flavourings and due to the fermentation process that takes place inside the bag, HorseHage has a sugar level of around 5% which is considerably lower than other forages. What's more, it is highly digestible, allowing efficient utilisation of the available nutrients and because it retains much of the value of fresh grass, it improves condition and adds a natural bloom to the horses' coats.

Turnout and stabling

- **The benefits** • **Summer and winter care**
- **The right rugs** • **Horsey hoodies**

The aim

If you have access to daily turnout, make the most of it – there are plenty of benefits. For example, if your young horse is fresh when competing, turnout takes the edge off him. I keep my youngsters out in the field at night – it means they may get dirty, and be more scruffy, but it helps to keep them quiet and content to ride and compete.

Bucas's ingenious zebra-striped fly rug

Turnout takes the edge off a fresh youngster

Summer care

During the event season, the stabled horses who are turned out after exercise wear Bucas rugs to keep them warm and clean, the thickness of which depends on the weather. And when there are flies around, they all wear Bucas's Buzz-Off Zebra fly rugs, the stripes of which are scientifically proven to repel flies which are deterred by the pattern. Plus, the rugs protect against the sun's harmful UV rays.

When they're in, they'll have a Bucas summer sheet underneath their main stable rug, because it's easier and quicker to wash a soiled summer sheet than it is a stable rug. It also means they'll have something clean against their skin.

Regular summer turnout means that at the end of the season, winding the horses down from peak fitness and turning them away for the winter is not such a shock to their system, because they're already used to going out. But if your horse is used to being stabled during the competition season, get him used to turnout by gradually increasing the time he spends out in the field each day.

My way

Even if the horses are still a bit damp having been washed down after exercise, we still rug them up straightaway and turn them out. Obviously, Bucas fly sheets are made of a breathable mesh, but all Bucas turnout rugs have a very clever Stay Dry lining which wicks away any moisture.

Say no to mud!

Horsey hoodies

When the stabled horses are turned out during the competition season, they'll also wear a Snuggy Hoods Turnout Hood, a great, all-round weatherproof hoody. They're made from a breathable, showerproof, stretchy fabric, lined with a silky shoulder and mane saver to prevent shoulder rub. Not only do they protect the horse from the mud and the weather, they can also be used to keep plaits in place the night before an event or to keep manes clean while travelling.

How to fit a hoody

Fit is important so if your horse is in-between sizes, choose the smaller size for a snugger fit. And don't worry about squeezing him into it – there's a knack! What you must do, however, is make sure your horse is clean, then if you have a hood with a zip, place the big opening over the horse's head and arrange the hood into position. Straighten the mane from the back of the hood, pass the belly band through the elastic strap and fasten tightly on the girth just behind the elbow – definitely no further back than that otherwise you'll reduce the length of the neck.

Next, move the adjustable Velcro on the nose to the correct width for your horse and check that when your horse puts his head down, the hood doesn't drag up into his eyes or over the withers.

For horses who aren't happy with their faces being covered, we also use the Headless Hoods for keeping the mud at bay. There are two fitting choices – a pull-on, which just slips over the nose and can be pulled back into position and a zipped option for easier fitting.

Winter plan

When the event season finishes in October, my horses have their shoes removed as long as my farrier, Nick Rule, agrees that their hooves are strong enough to cope. He says: "When the horses have their shoes off during this period, their feet will be trimmed every eight to 10 weeks – it depends on how their feet cope with the weather and the ground conditions."

Farrier Nick Rule – and Bailey

I'll also turn my horses out without any rugs until it gets very cold or unless it gets really wet. I believe they should live as naturally as possible, as that gives them the chance to grow a really thick coat. It may get muddy, but it builds up natural oils to keep them warm. Once the weather really sets in, I'll put them in Bucas rugs from the Power Turnout range. Fully clipped horses being turned out in cold weather will sometimes be double rugged.

The range has a clever climate control system in its Stay Dry lining, found in a variety of their rugs (stable, turnout, cooler) that can be put on a just-bathed or exercised horse and left on with no fear of the horse catching a chill. The lining wicks away the moisture and is always warm and dry next to the skin.

For best results

- As stable rugs get stained, we wash them on occasion. I don't have a commercial washing machine so on a fine day, Emma or Lauren will lie them down on the yard, get the hose out and scrub them by hand using non-bio detergent. They rinse the rugs thoroughly, then hang them somewhere to drip dry.

  However, the Snuggy Hoods hoodies are fully washable, so they can be popped into the washing machine.

Stabling – buy the best you can afford

Spring-clean

During the quieter times, we try to catch up with a few DIY jobs and give the yard a spring-clean – including any painting and repairs to the stables. Ascot Buildings supply my wooden stables and we paint the walls once or twice a year, depending on what the weather's been like and how much of a beating the preservative has taken from the sea mists that roll in.

It is important to have as good quality stabling as you can afford from a safety as well as a comfort aspect – and designs and materials that will stand the test of time. I was lucky when we started to design the yard because we already had some lovely old brick-built stables, so we wanted sympathetic designs that would complement them.

This is where Ascot Buildings were brilliant, helping us put together some designs and working with us to get exactly what we wanted that wouldn't look out of place with the existing outbuildings. And because we were starting from scratch with the new custom-built stabling, I was able to include my own finishing touches, such as kicking boards, two windows and metal strips across the door tops.

Inside the stables, I like kicking boards on the backs of the doors and metal strips on the tops of the stable doors. The strips help prevent the horses from chewing the wood and the metal plates on the outside of the doors are there to discourage them from scraping their teeth against the door. Part of the door jambs are also metal-covered to stop the horses chewing the wood, to keep everything neat and tidy and, most important of all, to preserve the horses' teeth.

If you decide to have windows in your horse's stable, it's important to make sure they are safe. Ideally, have a mesh wire on the inside, secured safely to the wall to prevent a horse putting his head through any glass or window covering.

Metal door strips prevent chewing

For best results

● We de-cobweb the stables on a regular basis – fitting it in when the horses are out being exercised. One of us will go in with a long brush to clean the walls, corners and ceiling to make sure the stables are tidy and dust-free.

Horsey haircuts

- **When to clip** - **How I clip**
- **Clipping tips** - **Trimming tails**

The aim

Removing all or part of your horse's coat depends on his workload and the way he is kept – for example, whether he's stabled, partly stabled or lives out 24/7. But clipping becomes a necessity during the winter months for working horses because it prevents unnecessary sweating caused by a thick coat, which can lead to difficult drying and possible chills.

How I clip

Once my horses have been in work for a few days after their winter holiday – and we've managed to get their coats clean – the clipping starts in early January. The stabled horses – and the six-year-olds who live out – have a full clip, but I leave their legs on and a half saddle patch. The five-year-olds have a blanket clip as they won't be working as hard as the more experienced horses.

Wear overalls or a jacket – loose hair clings to fleece

I'll trim around the edges of the ears and cut in a 3cm bridlepath behind the poll where the bridle sits. Any straggly hair over the top of the withers will be trimmed off and I like to keep the cat hairs under the chin under control. Manes, tails and forelocks are pulled so that they're easy to plait and always look smart.

I also trim the hair off around the top of the

When clipping, oil the blades every 10 minutes

coronet band to make a neat line and any feather off the heels, being careful not to cut the hair on the back of the fetlock joint, otherwise boots could rub.

Equipment

I use a clipper company called Clippersharp Ltd for all our clipping supplies. They are specialists in their field, and repair and supply new clippers and blades for virtually all makes of machines, as well as providing a blade-sharpening service.

Most blades need to be sharpened after three full clips, but sometimes sooner if the blades have been used on dirty coats. Clippers, on the other hand, need to be maintained regularly, particularly electrically-operated clippers, so it's essential to ensure they are safety tested and serviced each season to minimise any problems. We have ours sharpened and serviced by Clippersharp in the summer so we're prepared for that first clip.

For best results

- When clipping, bandage the tail and plait the mane over to keep all the hair out of the way.
- Mark out the clipping lines with chalk before you start.
- Apply a spray coat gloss before clipping to make the clippers glide easily through the hair.

My way

Once I've clipped a horse, I'll wipe him over completely with some warm water and a sponge or damp towel to get rid of excess grease.

Have someone to help you if it's your first time clipping – or your horse's. And if using mains-powered clippers, fit a circuit breaker.

Trimming tails

If a horse is sensitive about having his tail pulled, I use a Smart Grooming's Smart Tails humane thinning comb. Simply comb down the sides of the tail for a perfectly-pulled-tail look.

Is he fit for purpose?

- **The importance of fitness** ● **First farrier visit of the season**
- **Dental check-ups** ● **Coming back into work**

The aim

Fitness is a key factor in every horse's performance and the fitter a horse, the lower the risk of injury and the more he will enjoy his work. But if you're starting with an unfit horse, you need plenty of time to rebuild his fitness.

Allow time to build his fitness

Shoes on

Before I bring the horses back into work, my farrier – Nick Rule – will put their shoes back on. He says: "When horses come back into work after a break, the main focus is to make sure they're comfortable, and to remove any excess horn growth and 'flair' from the hoof wall to prevent cracks developing.

"The horses' feet will vary in condition depending on the quality of each horse's hooves. Some will be in reasonable condition, particularly if they have strong feet to start with, while others can develop cracks up the hoof wall, uneven growth, or even abscesses or bruising.

"In these cases, it's important to address these problems and deal with them appropriately to ensure comfort for the horse coming back into its working routine. If he is uncomfortable to start with, this can cause issues in his behaviour or ability to work in the early stages of his fitness regime."

Dental check-up

There are also factors my equine dentist, Keith Evans, considers: "When looking at a horse who's about to return to work, the first thing to consider is his general condition and appearance, how the

horse has been doing and what type of work he is about to start. I examine the horse in the stable and start by feeling the muscle groups on the head, the area behind the jaw and in front of the first vertebrae. I'm looking for balance and condition, which allows me to see if the horse is using both sides of his jaw when chewing. I'm also looking for any resistance when examined, as this may indicate discomfort in the soft tissue.

"I examine the front incisors before moving onto the molars/cheek teeth. I'm looking for effective chewing ability which means that he'll make the most of chewing his food to aid digestion. I then feel along the buccal and lingual edges of the molar arcades, dealing with any sharp enamel points that can come into conflict with the soft tissue of the cheeks and tongue, causing discomfort or distraction when bitted and ridden."

Equine dentist Keith Evans

Fitness diary

- **First three weeks** Roadwork on flat ground, then hills as the weeks progress. I start off with half-hour hacks and gradually build up to one hour approximately.
- **Weeks 3-4** Start to introduce schooling work, gradually building up the amount of work. Young horses would begin pole work and small jumping exercises.
- **Week 5** Start introducing some fast work, either on an all-weather gallop or in a field, preferably with a hill, which I prefer as the surface replicates a cross-country course. During the event season, the more mature horses (seven years-plus) do their fast work every third day. The five- and six-years-olds do their fast work every fourth or fifth day. I try to work it so that the final day of fast work is three days before the horse does an event.

Make sure your tack fits

The aim

It goes without saying that whatever the discipline, your clothing and your horse's kit must be comfortable and fit properly, especially the saddle. Mine is checked on a regular basis by a saddle fitter because my horses change shape during the season.

My saddle

My jumping saddle has a carbon-fibre tree with airbags rather than flocking. This helps eliminate any pressure points on the horse's back.

My kit and clothing

- **Choosing a saddle** ● **Bridle, bits and boots**
- **Essential extras** ● **My clothing**

Tack

● **Saddle/girth** A cross-country saddle should be cut well forward with very little knee roll and I like mine to have a low cantle that slopes away, so that when I move back, I am not tipped forward. Plenty of wither clearance is also important so that when the horse lands, the saddle doesn't pinch and restrict his movement when the pressure from the rider's weight goes onto the front of the saddle.

My jumping saddles have one flap instead of the usual two, which gives the feeling of being in close contact with my horse, which I like. However, if you're not used to this type of saddle, it might feel flimsy at first so practise riding in it at home before you compete. And I use a soft leather 'comfort' girth (below) that's padded, distributes pressure over a wider surface and is shaped so that when the front legs come back, the girth does not pinch and obstruct their movement.

● **Saddlecloth** I use PolyPads saddle pads under all my saddles and they're brilliant – not least because they're machine washable and look the part. And if fitted correctly, they don't slip.

For all three disciplines, I like saddle pads that are rounded at the front and square at the back corner – as in the Performer PolyPad so that when I'm working my horses, the loop of my reins doesn't get hooked around the front corner of the saddle pad.

The Performer is designed specifically for jumping, with cotton-rich towelling on the underside of each panel, enhancing the contact and the 'high-profile' cut along the spine being ideal for my higher-withered Thoroughbreds.

I've been using PolyPads for many years now, because they give excellent cushioning between the saddle and my horses' backs, providing comfort and enabling them to move unhindered. They're British-made and while they make different styles of saddle pads in all sorts of amazing colours, I use navy ones during exercise and training. Then during competition, the white ones look smart emblazoned with the embroidered logos of my sponsors. PolyPads saddle pads are available in over 240 different colour combinations, so are able to cater for almost anyone's competition colours.

I wash the pads on a regular basis. I find that a non-bio washing powder is best, because there's less chance of it causing rashes and irritation on the horse's skin.

● **Bridle/bits** I use a padded comfort bridle and flash noseband on all my horses. I start off with an eggbutt snaffle with or without a link (see photo below right, bottom left of picture). There is more of a nutcracker action without a link. Horses have different-shaped mouths and therefore have different requirements for the bit to be comfortable. With any gag or loose-ringed snaffle, I will fit rubber bit guards to avoid any pinching that may occur.

A snaffle bridle is my preferred choice

My bits

If a horse is too strong in a plain snaffle when he is jumping and galloping, I will try a Waterford. It is made up of a series of links that make it more difficult for a horse to lean on the bit and take a hold. If I need more brakes, I'll try a vulcanite pelham with a curb chain with a rubber cover, which I remove if I need a bit more response. I'd always use D-rings with one set of reins.

And for horses who 'draw down' from the contact, I'll use some sort of gag with up to three rings to encourage the horse to lift his head – the top ring being the least strong and the bottom being the most.

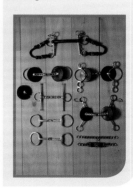

My way

I knot the end of the reins (below) so that if I have to slip them, it's easier to grab the little bump at the buckle than it is the reins.

While my horses don't wear over-reach boots for showjumping, they do for cross-country and I prefer the simple rubber type. However, I trim them so that they just cover the bulbs of the horse's front heels (below, right), to minimise the risk of him treading on the back of a front over-reach boot and tripping up.

● **Reins/martingale** My reins are grippy, rubber-covered leather for cross-country and showjumping. For dressage, I like leather 'laced' reins and prefer reins with buckles rather than billets, because they're more secure. I'll use a running martingale for cross-country and showjumping, fitted fairly loosely so that it only comes into play if my horse puts his head up high. I have two rubber rein stops on each rein – one to prevent the martingale ring getting caught up on the buckle at the bit end, the other to prevent the ring running up the rubber part of the reins. A martingale also doubles as a neck strap – good for grabbing at unexpected moments and better than 'catching' the horse in the mouth.

● **Leg protection** I've used New Equine Wear protective boots for over 15 years, so obviously they're a name I can trust. I use 'N.E.W' for all aspects of my horses' training – from hill work and hacking around the lanes at home in Devon, to flatwork, showjumping and cross-country, because they are specially designed to withstand the demands of cross country. For working the horses at home and for warming up for the dressage phase at an event, I use the 'Fleece' lined brushing boots on the front and back legs (pic 1), black ones at home and white ones at the bigger competitions. They're super-soft, meaning there's nothing that can rub or irritate the skin.

They provide exceptional comfort and are particularly good for horses with sensitive skin.

For the showjumping phase, I like N.E.W's open-fronted tendon boots on the front legs (pic 2). They have a solid shaped strip down the back of the tendons for protection in case a horse strikes into himself. The open front means if he does touch a pole, he'll feel it and will be more careful – which is why I prefer not to put boots on my horse's hindlegs for showjumping.

On the front legs for cross-country, I'll use fleece-lined boots with a protective strip down the back of the tendons (pic 3) and the 'Lite' orthopaedic foam-lined cross-country boots on the hindlegs (pic 4). As well as having a solid strip down the front of the boot to protect the cannon bone, these have an extra flap to protect the fetlock joint – unlike many other boots that are cut to finish just above the fetlock.

Then in the stables and when away at competitions, the horses wear Vent-Tex leg wraps. They help keep legs at optimum temperature and ease tired muscles, ligaments and tendons after competition. And I put them on the horses after wash-down, where the super-sort ventilating fabric helps wick away the moisture to allow the legs to dry naturally.

Ear muffs are useful on sharp horses

● **Ear muffs** I use ear muffs in the dressage phase to prevent flies bothering the horses through a test. William Fox-Pitt recommended I use them on a sharp horse when I went across country, because the wind whistling past their ears can upset and excite them. It really can make a difference to some horses.

SupaStuds

● **Studs** My horses always wear studs when I'm jumping on grass, be it showjumping or cross-country, to help prevent slips and slides through turns which can knock a horse's confidence. And the general rule is that the firmer the ground, the smaller and more pointed the studs need to be. Heavier ground, on the other hand, requires bigger, chunkier studs.

I've used SupaStuds (above) for a number of years and will put two in each shoe. These award-winning, patented studs have a unique, self-cleaning design that enables them to be screwed straight into a standard stud hole without first having to use a tap to clear the thread.

Additional advantages include a recess at the base of the SupaStud, removing a potentially problematic pressure point; careful design of the stud's leading edge, making it less likely that the stud will cross-thread when you're inserting it; and the ability to screw the stud in flush to the shoe, effectively 'locking' it into place. The whole stud is hardened, making it last longer and, as a result of the hardening, it is very resistant to rust.

Rider clothing

Up to Novice level, I wear a hacking jacket with a coloured stock, beige Ariat breeches and Ariat gloves. But at Intermediate level and above, I wear a navy blue jacket with a white stock and white Ariat breeches. And while I know it might sound a bit old-fashioned, I wear my stock cross-country as I like to have something around my neck to make it feel stable.

I think that Ariat have made a huge impact on the equestrian world over the past 20 years and are fast becoming a favourite choice of riders

when it comes to footwear and rider clothing – from the grassroots riders to the professionals. Ariat has cleverly combined style and function, both on and off the horse, with cutting-edge technology, comfort and durability.

● **Breeches** Ariat's technological developments spans its entire equestrian range, including my favourite Olympia breeches. What I like about them is their 'comfortability' factor, which is all down to the four-way stretch fabric that makes them comfortable to wear all day long. What's more, an elastic 'V' panel in the back waistband gives plenty of stretch to accommodate a rider's varying hip angles – for example, as they're galloping and jumping. And their unique Calf Fit System gives a streamlined appearance – after all, there's nothing worse than bulk in your boots!

● **Boots** My favourite day-to-day boots are the Bromont. They come with a full-length back zip in insulated and non-insulated versions, which means boots for all seasons. They incorporate ATS technology which results in a cleverly engineered footbed that offers cushion, comfort and helps reduce stress in the foot and lower leg.

And when I'm walking the course, a pair of good all-rounder Coniston boots are never far from my boot rack at home. With their lace-up, smart-casual country style, they're good enough to ride in and be seen in socially!

Ariat combine style with practicality

My advice

Gatehouse recommends that riding hats should be replaced following a severe impact or fall. The inner protective lining is designed to absorb and disperse the impact but while the hard outer shell may retain its shape, the EPS (polystyrene) liner becomes compressed, reducing the shock absorption properties and rendering the hat less effective in future.

For best results

● Make sure that the same person puts on a horse's boots – whether it's brushing, open-fronted tendon or cross-country boots, otherwise there could be a variety of tensions which could cause injury.

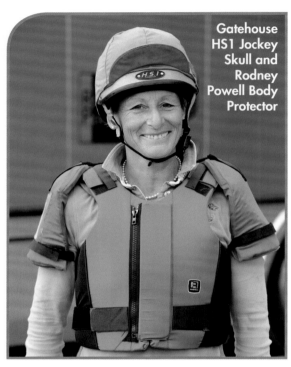

Gatehouse HS1 Jockey Skull and Rodney Powell Body Protector

● **Hat** For dressage, showjumping or everyday wear at home, my helmet of choice is the BSEN1384-approved Gatehouse Conquest, a lightweight, ventilated helmet with a removable, washable liner that comes into its own in summer.

As for cross-country, I've long been a fan of the Snell-approved Gatehouse HS1 Jockey Skull. Snell E2001 is the highest helmet safety standard currently in manufacture and includes a unique test that simulates a rider falling into a fence rail or having a secondary hit by a horse's hoof, making it a sound choice when jumping fixed fences. The HS1 is also reinforced with carbon fibre around the lower edge which offers increased crush resistance over this vulnerable area.

Riding hat manufacturers are constantly striving to improve the level of protection available, while producing a hat that is comfortable to wear. The introduction of a polystyrene (EPS) liner has played a big part in that development process, since it is lightweight and also provides excellent levels of shock absorption.

● **Body armour** Body protectors are an established piece of kit for event riders, constructed of panels or blocks or heat-responsive, shock-absorbent foam with a fabric outer and mesh lining. A body protector may feel stiff at cooler temperatures but a close fit will allow body heat to penetrate the foam, making it more flexible.

I wear Rodney Powell Body Protectors that are approved to BETA Level 3, the most commonly used standard for most equestrian disciplines. But whichever brand or design of hat or body protector you choose, it must fit well and be correctly adjusted to be both comfortable and give the maximum level of protection. Therefore, it's advisable to buy from a retailer with trained fitting staff. They can advise on the correct hat standard to suit your riding activity, fine-tune the fit if necessary and adjust the harness. Trained fitters will also ensure you have the correct size of body armour and explain how to adjust it so the guide marks at shoulder and waist are covered.

I never ride without my Point Two Air Jacket

I wear a Point Two Air Jacket on top of my body protector which inflates if you fall off, and I would never ride without one – even when schooling youngsters over cross-country fences. When you first wear one, it might feel like extra baggage but once you're galloping along, you don't notice it at all. And besides, they certainly take the sting out of some potentially nasty falls – and I should know!

It's competition day!

Follow my management guidelines for success at the event...

- On the day of a competition, keep your horse's routine as normal as possible by giving him his usual hay and hard feed while you're getting ready in the morning, then a haynet to travel with.
- Check your horse regularly on a journey, making sure he stays at a comfortable temperature. As much fresh air as possible is best for him, so open more windows and add another rug, rather than close the windows to keep him warm. Don't over-rug him... remember, sweat drains energy. Offer him water regularly, especially in hot weather.

Unload your horse and let him have a graze

- Arrive in plenty of time. Unload your horse, take his travel boots off and let him get his head down to pick at some grass. This is important because he will have travelled with his head up, so any mucus needs to drain away.

Lunge him if he's fresh

- If he's fresh, lunge him for 10-15 minutes before you ride to settle him.
- Take a skip with you to clean out the lorry or trailer on arrival and during the day, so that you have a tidy work place around the lorry in case visiting owners drop by.

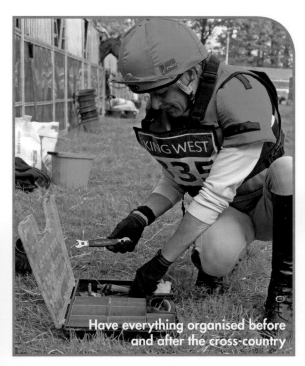
Have everything organised before and after the cross-country

- Before you leave for your cross-country round, make sure that all your gear is within easy reach when you return – for example, make sure that buckets are filled and kept out of the sun; sponges, sweat scraper, headcollar and lead rope, cooler, haynet, stud box and towels are to hand.
- Offer water right up to the moment you leave for a cross-country round so that your horse does not become thirsty or try to drink a lot in one go. My horses always have access to a haynet, too, which is a good way to keep them relaxed in the lorry. I take it away about half-an-hour before a big run so that they aren't galloping with a full, heavy belly. Research suggests, however, that galloping on an empty stomach can be bad for horses, particularly those with gastric ulcers, as acid splashes around in their stomach. A lining of food prevents this from happening.

My way

Once I've lunged a fresh horse at a competition, I'll put him back on the lorry for about half-an-hour. That's usually enough time for him to settle and calm down before I ride him.

If you get straight on-board a fresh horse, you run the risk of both getting tense and falling out with each other. But some time spent on the lunge allows an excitable horse to have a bit of a play – a buck and a squeak – to help him get rid of any pent-up energy.

Starting a youngster

- **Scales of Training** • **Voice aids**
- **Lungeing** • **Straightness, bend and transitions**

The aim

Every rider wants to do the best for their horse and when it comes to training, this is no exception. So to help you get the most from your horse, think about the way you train him. Rush and you could find yourself back at square one, but take your time and you'll find it's the best way to secure a solid foundation on which to build for the future.

The Scales of Training is a training system designed to help riders understand what they should be aiming for in their training. They consist of six stages, the idea being to work through them all gradually, whether your horse is Novice or Advanced and whether you compete regularly or are happy just schooling at home.

Rhythm
This relates to the regularity of the basic paces.

Suppleness and softness
The horse should be free from physical and mental tension, working with a swinging, relaxed back.

Contact and connection
The contact between the horse's mouth and rider's hands should be consistent but elastic.

Impulsion
This is the energy created by the hindlegs, which should be transmitted into forward movement.

Straightness
This helps to develop both sides of the horse, said to be 'straight' when his forehand (shoulder) is in line with his hindquarters.

Collection and engagement
This is achieved as the horse carries more weight on his hindquarters by stepping under more with his hindleg. It lightens the shoulder for more freedom of movement and improves his balance.

The first stages

To start a young horse, I'll usually back him when he's three years old, once he's used to having a headcollar on and being led. I'll start by lungeing him off a headcollar in an enclosed area, teaching him to walk, trot and obey my voice, as he needs to learn the vocal aids such as 'walk on' and 'trot on'. He must also learn to come back to walk to a 'whoa', and to stand and not turn in towards me. It takes a few days for him to do this confidently, with me being methodical in correcting him if he does anything wrong and rewarding him with my voice when he's good.

Lungeing is an invaluable discipline of any horse's schooling routine, whatever his experience. With an experienced horse (see Imperial Cavalier, below), you can work him in a different outline depending on where you attach the side-reins. Attach them to the girth for a longer, lower outline and to encourage the horse to stretch down or to the saddle's D-rings for an outline that's more 'up'. Always use side-reins with an elastic section, with the inside side-rein two holes shorter than the outside rein.

Lower outline

'Up' outline

Under saddle

Teach your horse the principles of straightness and bend, and the importance of correct transitions…

Straightness

To work on your horse's straightness, ensure that he moves forward with good impulsion and accepts the bit with a consistent, elastic rein contact. There should be no resistance to the hand and his head should be positioned just in front of the vertical with the poll the highest point of the neck. He must travel in a completely straight line, equal in both hands.

For a horse to be straight, his head and chest must be in front of hindlegs that follow the front legs. He must not be allowed to drift to one side, nor travel with his hindquarters crooked, but should stay straight as he travels forward into the rein, with the rider supporting him equally with both legs to maintain the straightness. Bear in mind, straightness is an ongoing process – without continual work, the horse will revert to his natural crookedness.

Straightness requires continual work

My way

When lungeing a young horse, I'll have some horse and pony nuts in my pocket to reward him when he's responded positively to what I ask of him. This encourages him to think of you as his friend, even though you're asking him to do some strange, unfamiliar things!

Bend

By nature, a horse will not travel around a corner or make a turn with an inside bend – instead, he'll try to fall in with his inside shoulder. So you must teach him how to balance and maintain a consistent length bend through his body, from nose to tail. This training principle must become second nature to him but if you allow him to make a mistake without correcting it, it will be more difficult to put right. And this will have a knock-on effect when riding more difficult movements at a higher level.

So as you approach the corner, ask for a small amount of bend with your inside rein, supporting him with your inside leg on the girth. As you reach the corner, keep your inside leg at the girth to keep his ribcage out slightly, his shoulder upright and inside hindleg activated. Keep a supporting outside rein, and ensure he has the correct length bend through his body and shows a smooth curve on the line you're riding. Then practise turning onto the centre line and three-quarter lines, thinking of using the inside leg to outside rein as you ride each corner.

Transitions

A transition is a change in the way the horse moves – when he changes speed or stride length, when moving from one movement to another. Correctly ridden transitions will improve a horse's balance, suppleness, obedience to the aids and collection.

When your young horse starts his ridden training, introduce all transitions gradually,

Keep his inside hindleg activated

teaching him correct upward and downward transitions through all three gaits – for example, from walk to trot, trot to canter, from canter to trot, then back to walk. For the horse to understand the aids for the transitions, however, make sure that you can apply and co-ordinate the aids correctly and consistently.

Common mistake

● When turning, do not allow your horse to fall in through the shoulder.

Solution To discourage this from happening, keep a contact on the outside rein, make sure he obeys the inside leg pressure and doesn't fall in. Keep your outside leg positioned behind the girth (left). This helps prevent the hindquarters from kicking out, keeping them in line on the curve of the corner. Start this at walk, then progress to trot.

Keep a contact on the outside rein

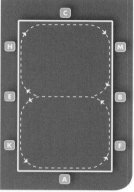

For best results

● When your horse is balanced through the corners, trot left around the arena. Turn left at B (above), ride across the centre line to E, turn right at E. Ride around to B and turn right, across the centre line then turn left at E.

This is good for control, producing correct turns, riding with your horse's body straight before you prepare to turn the other way. The key to success is to prepare for the turn and while it sounds obvious, really ride the turn. And change your trot diagonal across the centre line by sitting for one stride.

Perfect your
posture

The rider's position

- **Schooling mirrors** ● **Sitting up straight**
- **Legs and hands** ● **Improving the seat**

The aim

As well as the horse being straight in his way of going, the rider must also be straight. Having the correct posture on a horse is essential, for if the rider is crooked or rides with a collapsed hip, this will impact on the horse and make it difficult for him to go correctly. What's more, it's a common riding problem so this is when a rider can always benefit from having another pair of eyes on the ground to help them – an experienced friend or a trainer, for example.

Mirror, mirror

If you frequently school on your own at home, investing in training mirrors for your arena is common sense and money well spent – after all, approximately 65% of the population are visual learners. Using mirrors provides instant visual feedback, allowing corrections to be made at the time, enabling you to improve and get the most from each training session. Not only will they benefit your own riding position – whatever level you ride at – but you'll be able to tell if your horse is working correctly too.

My mirrors come from Mirrors for Training and I use them to check my straightness and that of the horse, and his general way of going. For example, are his hindlegs in line with his front legs or are his hindquarters slightly crooked? Are my own feet and shoulders level? Are my hands level and still? Once you can see that both horse and rider are straight, make a mental note how it feels so that you can practise this feeling when you're working in the field or out hacking.

This instant feedback you get from seeing your horse's outline, your seat and application of the aids and any inaccuracies in your schooling means that errors can be rectified immediately before they become habit forming. What's more, mirrors in the arena can help boost the understanding and technique of a particular movement or the horse's way of going, enabling the rider to see what the judge or trainer can see.

Another option is to ask a friend to film your schooling session on a video camera – or even a mobile phone, which can also be of huge benefit. Playing it back, and assessing your riding position and analysing your horse's way of going may highlight some mistakes you may not have realised you're making. Remember, the camera never lies!

Too far forward

Too far back

Sit up straight!

Keep on checking that you're sitting correctly with a nice straight back, head up and shoulders back. If ever I need a reminder to sit properly, I always think back to a piece of advice dressage rider Carl Hester gave me a few years ago – that is, to make the front of your body longer. I feel that is better than telling yourself to sit up straight, because making the front of your body longer will prevent you from leaning forward and looking down, which is a common fault of many riders.

On the other hand, don't get so fixated on sitting up straight that you end up leaning too far back, because having pressure on the back of the saddle is uncomfortable for the horse. And in focusing on sitting up straight, don't forget about the position of your legs and hands.

Elongate your front

My way

I would encourage riders to have as much training as possible, certainly when starting out and if they're competing and continuing to progress up the levels. Riding is an ongoing learning process and even I, at this stage in my career, have some training help. I have dressage lessons with trainer Ferdi Eilberg, who makes sure I'm riding correctly and effectively and picks up any bad habits I may be falling into.

I very much rely on Ferdi, as I do Tracie Robinson, Team GBR's Performance Dressage (Eventing) Coach. And it's useful now that my daughter Emily is more experienced because she can spot any bad habits starting.

Legs

Sit in the centre of the saddle with a soft knee – no tightness or gripping allowed! Your lower leg should wrap softly around the sides of your horse, hanging heavy with its weight in the heel of your boots and your toes up. Don't force the heels down, as this can unbalance you.

Learn to be quiet with your lower leg, because it's easy to use it too much without realising. Then the horse's sides become less sensitive – ie, dead to the leg – and he becomes reliant on you nudging away all the time to keep him going.

Instead, he must learn to be responsive to your leg aids so keep your leg still and soft until you need to create more impulsion. For example, if riding an upward transition to trot, just close your legs against the horse's sides. If there's no reaction, be quick with your lower leg and administer a sharp kick – ie, a small bit of pressure to get a

response. When you do this, keep your reins soft so that if your horse does jump forward, the energy has somewhere to go and he's not reprimanded with a tug on a restricting rein. Reward him with your voice and/or a pat when he responds. Remember, the rider should ride from the legs and seat to the hand. The rider's legs create the energy, encouraging the horse forward into the contact, while the hands channel and control that energy.

The horse should then come into a correct outline by engaging the hindleg and softening into the rein, working over a relaxed topline (back and neck) into the contact. But it's a common fault of many riders to think that if they 'fix' their horse's head down with their hands, he's on the bit. However, all this does is pull his head in, making for a very short neck, an unengaged hindleg and him 'running on' and becoming hollow.

Channel the energy

Hands

Generally speaking, the rider's hands must be used in conjunction with the legs. Bear in mind that relentless pulling and tugging on a sensitive mouth is neither good for horse nor human – it can lead to resistance and a battle of wills which the horse, given his size, is always going to win. And the more you pull, the more you will find that your horse will become dead in the mouth (numb). Instead, a gentle vibration with your fingers on the rein should be all that's needed to encourage sensitivity in the contact.

Some riders have naturally good hands – a good 'feel' – and it's that sympathetic, quiet hand that you're trying to achieve. Therefore, remember to keep your hands still with your thumbs on top, carrying them slightly forward and up in front of you.

You should also have a good angle in your arms, with your elbows relaxed and close to your sides. There should also be a nice straight line from the elbows through to your wrists, hands and rein to the horse's mouth. The straighter your arms, the more rigid and tense the rein will feel to your horse. However, the more angle you have in your elbows, the more flexible and forgiving you can be with the rein, so there's less chance of your horse resisting against the hand.

Improving your balance

While you may expect your horse to be athletic and beautifully balanced, think about how balanced you are in the saddle. While you may spend many hours schooling – and on both reins to make sure your horse is evenly muscled on both sides of his body – if you don't sit straight or aren't strong enough to hold yourself correctly in the saddle, what chance has your horse got? So from time to time, check that you're not hanging on to the reins to help you balance, which is a common fault among younger and less experienced riders.

To check your balance in the saddle, give and retake the reins. Do this by giving your hands forward towards the horse's mouth so that your reins form a slight loop, then take them back. This exercise will remind you not to hang on to your horse's mouth, something you must be aware of.

This is also a good test to check how much self-carriage he has – ie, carrying his own body weight and not leaning on the rein contact for support. When he has learnt true engagement, he should keep the same outline he had before you gave the rein forward, neither going behind the bit nor hollowing (putting his head up). A more novice horse will open his neck a bit when you do this exercise, but should be happy to come back into an outline when you retake your reins.

My way

To help a young or inexperienced horse achieve better balance – and to keep an Advanced horse supple and on top of his game – riding lots of transitions and changes of direction during their everyday schooling sessions is the way forward. In fact, I remember reading that Carl Hester rides about 200 transitions each training session! Don't forget, however, that a young horse will get tired so from time to time, allow him breaks to stretch down.

Keep your hands still

Give and retake the reins

Lungeing helps

It can be an important training discipline to be taught on the lunge, where the rider doesn't have to think about controlling their horse, but can concentrate more on perfecting their position in the saddle – and ideally on a quiet, unflappable horse. And there are mounted exercises you can try to help improve your posture...

● If you're going to be lunged without stirrups, either take them off the saddle or cross them over in front of the pommel, so that they can't interfere with anything you're doing in the saddle. The main benefit of riding without stirrups is to encourage a rider who gets tense and grips with their knees to sit deep in the saddle. Doing so will gradually help them to relax and absorb the movement of the gaits, especially the trot and canter, without being bounced up and down.

● If you're lunged without reins, make a knot in them so that they're well out of harm's way. Lungeing without reins not only helps the rider to develop better balance and a secure, independent seat to prevent them from holding onto the reins and relying on them to balance their own body, but confidence in the saddle too. So try placing your hands on your hips; moving your upper body from side to side; placing your hands on your head; or raising your arms out to the sides of your body and circling them.

● Another exercise to help you sit deeper in the saddle – when your horse is stationary – involves holding onto the pommel, lifting both legs away and allowing them to drop down and hang loose. Then once you're established doing this, let go and do it without holding onto the pommel.

Lungeing helps improve the rider's position

Understand the
basic principles

Basic dressage skills

- **Serpentines** ● **Transitions**
- **How to halt** ● **Effective exercises**

The aim

When you ride the dressage phase at the lower levels of eventing, the tests all require you to show your ability to ride some simple basic requirements of dressage. For example, you must be able to ride straight on straight lines, with a bend through corners, circles and serpentines, and to show smooth transitions between the different paces.

Practice makes perfect

What can really help put you at the top of your game when it comes to riding a dressage test at a competition is the training you put in beforehand – either in an arena or a paddock at home, or at your livery yard. Schooling sessions riding in a 40 x 20 or 60 x 20-metre arena – depending on whether you're riding at Novice or a higher level – is time well spent. And always know where your markers are, and ride to them.

Even if you're lucky enough to have a school at home, try riding in a field from time to time using push-in dressage markers to map out your arena. It's amazing how wobbly a horse can feel if he's not used to working in a field without the security of a fence to support him! I also think it's beneficial to work on grass, because there are usually more distractions that help replicate a competition feel.

When I school in the field in a marked-out arena, I tend to put the corner markers – K, H, M and F – slightly closer to the short side than they'd be in an arena. This encourages you to ride the corners accurately and the better you ride them, the more the horse gets used to the balance needed around a deeper corner.

Then when you ride in a 'normal' arena at a competition, you should feel as if you have more room to make the turn. If riding along the short side then turning across the diagonal, for example, you'll have more time to prepare and the horse's balance should be better – this is because you've both been used to riding sharper, deeper, more angled corners at home.

Serpentines

Once your horse has learnt to travel around a corner in balance, he can then progress to serpentines in walk and trot, which are just as much a skill for the rider to master as they are for the horse, as everything happens very quickly!

It's customary to start with a three-loop serpentine (below, left), paying particular attention to riding the correct shape. This movement needs a lot of care to ensure that all the loops are equal in depth and shape. Serpentines are an important training exercise that help your horse become supple and more manoeuvrable. So practise riding half-circles with a correct inside bend, linking them together across the centre with straight lines. Irregular curves joined by nearly diagonal lines will lose you marks in a dressage test!

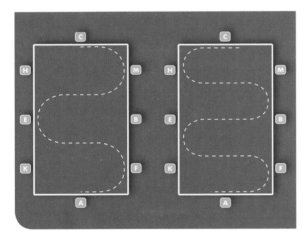

Pay attention to the size and shape of each loop, making them equal and ensuring you change your trot diagonal across the centre line – this will help your horse to rebalance. You must insist on the correct bend around each loop and make sure that you ride the serpentines in both directions – ie, starting on the left rein and then on the right. As the three-loop serpentine becomes easier for your horse, progress to riding four (above, right) and then five-loop serpentines.

Transitions

Once a horse is supple on each rein through the turn, riding transitions is an exercise I practise with all my horses – from the youngsters to the advanced horses – as a sort of 'bread and butter' exercise!

Walk-trot transition

This is the first transition your horse will have to master, so he must learn to be responsive to the leg aid. Equally important, however, is the preparation you must make before you ask him for the transition so that you don't spring it on him. So at walk, prepare to trot by shortening your reins, gathering the walk up and applying a bit of pressure from your lower leg. Give your horse a soft rein to go into (don't pull back or you'll send him conflicting signals) but if he's young or inexperienced, don't be surprised if the transitions aren't perfectly balanced to start with or if he doesn't respond immediately to your leg aid.

Common mistake Walk-trot

● Your horse resists the hand and lifts his head as you ask him to trot.

Solution Do not go into trot. Instead, bring your horse back to walk immediately, ask for more roundness with lowered and widened hands, ask for the transition again. If he lifts his head again, walk, ask for even more roundness, then ask again.

If necessary, keep repeating until he goes forward into the trot transition, maintaining the correct outline – at which point reward him immediately with your voice or a pat with your inside hand. Then continue in trot.

Be as quick as possible to correct any errors and follow the same procedure if your horse lowers his head. Bring him back to walk, lift his head up by raising your hands, then try again. This time, however, keep your hands slightly higher and vibrate your fingers as you ask for trot.

My way

In the walk-trot transition, if you have had to repeat the transition and helped your horse by either lowering and widening your hands (if he lifted his head up) or raising your hands (if he dipped his head down) – and he has responded positively – next time you ask for the transition, bring your hands up to the correct position, together in front of you and slightly in front of the pommel.

Make sure that you're not made to ride with your hands in a certain position to prevent your horse from making a mistake – he has to make the mistake, so that you can correct it and that he learns from his error. It's very easy to end up riding the horse the way he wants you to ride him.

Trot-walk transition

When making any downward transitions, prepare your horse a few steps before asking for the transition. Do this by drawing your upper body back a little which signals to the horse that you want him to slow down.

For the trot-walk transition, slightly close your hands on the reins and keep your leg on because this will encourage your horse to go forward into the downward transition, not fall onto his forehand (shoulder). Remember that preparation is key.

Keep your leg on to maintain the hindleg activity as your horse comes into walk. Otherwise, if you just apply some pressure to the reins, your horse is likely to 'fall' into the walk – pulling down onto the forehand into walk – rather than going 'forward' into the transition.

Prepare for the transition

Take your upper body slightly back

For best results

- A series of easy-to-ride exercises will test his and your responses, and highlight any areas of sluggishness.

  For example, when practising your walk-trot, trot-walk transitions, from rising trot come back to walk for three or four strides before picking up the trot again. Be strict with yourself and your horse to make sure you learn to execute these transitions accurately and that your horse does exactly as you ask.

Trot-canter transition

Once the walk-trot, trot-walk transitions have become nice and fluid, progress to the trot-canter, canter-trot transitions, for which preparation is imperative. Obviously the horse should be established in the canter and be able to maintain it for a simple exercise that includes canter on a circle, followed by canter in a straight line, then on a circle again.

As you prepare for the transition in rising trot, make sure that your horse has the correct length bend through his body from nose to tail. Then sit to the trot and apply your leg aids – inside leg on the girth, outside leg behind – with your upper body straight and your shoulders back (right). Ride 'up' into the transition, keeping a soft contact on the rein. If your horse lifts or lowers his head, apply the same procedure as for the walk-trot transition.

For the downward transition, bring your upper body back, keep your leg on, then close your hands on the reins.

To test your horse's balance and obedience to the aids, as well as your application of them, come back from canter to trot for six strides, then pick up canter again. You can also vary the number of strides to see how quickly he responds to your aids.

Walk-canter transition

This transition should come easily to the horse if he understands the 'canter on' aid. Make sure the walk is active and that your horse is condensed in his frame at walk. When you ask for the transition, sit square with your upper body upright, inside leg on the girth and your outside leg behind it. This may take some practice but insist he goes cleanly from walk to canter, otherwise allowing him to put in half a trot stride could become a habit.

Canter-walk transition

This can take longer to establish and to perform it well the horse must become engaged, 'sitting' on his hindquarters with the hindlegs well underneath him. He must also be able to carry

Ride 'up' from trot to canter

himself in self-carriage and canter with a short, collected stride.

First practise this transition off a turn – canter down the long side of the arena, then turn across the school from E or B (below right), bringing your horse to walk as you approach the centre line. Do this by bringing your upper body back and closing your hands on both reins – your horse should then drop into a nice, forward walk. Keep your leg on during the transition, so that he doesn't just collapse onto the forehand.

Making a canter-walk transition off a turn like this will encourage engagement of the hindleg in readiness for the walk transition. So practise this transition on both reins, initially from turns into the walk then as it becomes more established, ask for the transition on a straight line.

For best results

- When teaching a young or inexperienced horse the canter-walk transition, I initially allow him one or two trot strides before coming into the walk. This gives him more of a chance to balance himself while he is still learning about engagement and becoming stronger in his frame.

● When working on transitions, also work on keeping your horse straight. Do this by laying a few poles parallel to each other around your arena or field, set 1 metre apart. As you ride through them, make your transition – the poles will help keep your horse straight through his body. Ride some transitions between the poles and some after so that your horse doesn't anticipate where you're going to ask for them.

The same goes for transitions on a circle – always ask for them in different places, otherwise your horse could anticipate them. So vary where you ask for the transitions to keep your horse fresh and alert.

Stay straight

How to halt

Once the walk, trot and canter transitions have become smooth and correct, start working on the halt then the more advanced transitions of halt into trot and trot into halt. For these, however, your horse must have learnt more about engagement and how to push from the hindleg.

Engagement involves the horse learning to shift his weight from the front end of his body to the back – from the forehand to the hindquarters. A young horse will naturally use his hindlegs to push his body forward, which is what causes him to be 'on the forehand'. With training, however, he will gradually learn to step under more, taking more weight onto his hindlegs by lowering his hindquarters which then lifts and lightens the forehand, improving his balance.

As far as the halt is concerned, you're looking for your horse to come into a square halt. A young horse, however, will have no idea what he's meant to be doing to begin with so start by accepting any halt from him – just as long as he comes into it smoothly, without resistance, stays straight and stands still which is important.

Don't be surprised either if a youngster comes into the halt leaving a hindleg out. This is quite common in the early stages of a young horse's career and one who hasn't learnt about engagement and self-carriage. It's all you can expect at this stage so as long as he's standing still, ask him to 'step up' with that stray hindleg.

To do this, keep a contact on the reins to prevent your horse from walking forward then with your heel (left if his left hindleg is out and right for the right hindleg), nudge him to step forward with that particular leg. If he steps forward too much, don't worry – as long as he responds to your aid, that's what you're looking for. Then praise him with a pat.

As the halt becomes more established with his outline rounder and engagement improved – and if you've been consistent in asking him to step up with the trailing hindleg – he will find it easier to come into a square halt on a consistent basis.

Keep him round in the halt

● There are a few things to remember when riding a halt on the centre line. For example, if your trot is too big or too fast, your horse will be unbalanced going into the halt, instead of being collected to achieve better balance.

Try to adjust any wiggles or drifting by using your legs equally and with an even contact in both reins. Thinking more leg but less hand, and riding forward up the centre line helps with straightness. Alternatively, imagine you're riding down a tube with the walls helping to keep you nice and straight.

Trot-halt requires engagement

Checking the halt

If you're lucky enough to have training mirrors in your school – I have them positioned down one long side and both short sides of my arena at home – practise your halts in front of them so that you can see clearly the position of your horse's legs underneath you.

Although you're advised not to look down at your horse's legs, I think that if you don't have mirrors you won't know whether you're correcting him correctly if he has left a leg out to the side. It would be easy for your horse to get in a muddle if you're trying to correct one hindleg when it's actually the other that needs bringing into line.

Canter-halt

The canter-halt transition isn't performed until Advanced level, when horses are more engaged. However, it's a good idea to stretch the boundaries because at home you should always be working your horse at a level higher than the one at which you're competing. This takes the pressure off the horse and rider at a competition, because you'll both be familiar and more comfortable with a lower-level movement if you're used to working at a higher level at home.

Make sure, however, that your horse doesn't pull down on the rein as he comes into the halt and ends up on the forehand. He should sit nicely on his hocks and be in front of the leg as you ask for the halt. Encourage him also to stay straight – check in your mirrors if you have them and correct your horse if he's crooked. Or ask a friend or your trainer to be your eyes on the ground.

Don't forget
the walk!

Why walk's important

- **The different walks** - **Showing a difference**
- **Doing it my way** - **Common problems solved**

The aim

Walk is a pace that's often forgotten about during schooling sessions, but it appears in dressage tests at all levels. It's very easy to lose marks for the various walks if they're not practised at home.

The walk is a marching pace, a four-beat gait that averages about 4mph and follows the sequence of left hindleg, left front leg, right hindleg, right front leg. As a horse walks, he moves his head and neck up and down slightly and this helps him balance.

How to ride it

There are four variations of the walk – medium, free walk on a long rein, extended and collected – each requiring the rider to maintain a consistent but elastic rein contact.

Medium

This is the 'regular' walk where the horse walks purposefully with even steps and with the hind feet landing in or in front of the hoofprints of the front feet – this is called 'tracking up'. 'Overtracking' is when the hind feet land in front of the hoofprints made by the front feet. The horse should maintain a correct outline and the rider's hands should follow the natural movement of the horse as he moves his head forward and back as he walks.

Follow the movement in medium walk

Did you know?

- The difference between a free walk on a long rein and an extended walk is that for a free walk, the horse's head and neck are stretched down lower and more forward in front than in the extended walk.
- It is thought that the walk is the gait that promotes muscular development in the horse more than the other gaits.

Free walk on a long rein

You'll come across this movement at Novice and Intermediate levels. It's a pace in which the horse must lower and stretch out his head and neck, but it's easy to throw away valuable marks if your free walk is not up to scratch. So teach a horse the free walk by first working him on a circle at a good medium walk, holding him together in an outline.

From that walk, ask him to go into a free walk on a long rein by encouraging him to stretch his head and neck forward and down – help him to do this by lowering and widening your hands. Once he has stretched down, pat him before gathering up the reins and picking him up again.

Then work your horse in an extra-short outline at walk for a few steps, before asking again for the free walk and allowing him to draw the rein out. You're aiming for a forward stretching outline, a good open stride, a lengthened topline and a neck that is positioned below the level of the withers. However, remember to maintain a consistent feel on your horse's mouth, keeping the contact, with no baggy reins allowed!

Next, gather up the reins to make the transition back to medium walk. As you do so, keep your leg on to encourage your horse to continue marching on forward, which should result in a smooth seamless transition and no resistance to the hand.

To help my horses really understand the difference between the walks, I'll alternate between medium walk, free walk on a long rein, medium walk, then back to free walk on a long rein. This will encourage them to focus on the rider's aids and show a real difference between the different walks.

Allow him to stretch in the free walk

For best results

● It is easier to teach your horse to stretch down while you're on a circle – for example, when perfecting the medium walk to a free walk on a long rein. But you will need to practise over a number of days for improved results.

Also encouraging your horse to relax and take the rein down in walk – after he has finished his schooling session, on the bit in an outline, having worked through different paces and movements – is almost a natural progression for him. By this stage, he'll be ready to relax and want to stretch, so you'll be halfway to achieving the correct outline needed for a free walk on a long rein.

From time to time when I'm schooling my horses, I allow them a short walk or trot break to stretch down over the topline before picking up the pace again. I think this is very important. Remember that when the horse is working in an outline and performing various dressage movements, his muscles can tire and get sore, which can lead to resistance and him not enjoying what he's doing.

Extended walk

Once you reach Intermediate and Advanced levels, you'll have to ride an extended walk in your dressage test. This is when your horse must cover as much ground as possible with each walk stride, overtracking and without losing the regularity of his steps. His poll should be lowered and at a similar level to his withers, his nose out in front of the vertical and he should walk on with as long and as purposeful a stride as possible – but not a quicker stride.

Collected walk

In this, the horse should be working well from behind – from engaged hindlegs through to a consistent but elastic rein contact. The horse's neck should be raised and arched, with the horse carrying his own weight in 'self-carriage'. The pace should stay marching, not hurried and irregular, but each step should be slightly higher and cover less ground than the medium walk. Although the collected walk is shorter than the medium walk, it shows more activity.

Common mistakes The walk

● The horse doesn't stretch forward and down enough in the free walk and the extended walk.
Solution Practise overstretching your horse at home. On a 20-metre circle, ride your horse in an outline so he is more ready to want to stretch and relax. Lean forward a little, lower and widen your hands and encourage him to stretch down and round. If you're in a field, even allow him to have a nibble of grass as a reward. Then pick him up into an outline for a while, before repeating the stretch.

● He's lacking purpose in the walk and not tracking up or overtracking.
Solution He must stay in front of the leg and march on, so give him a sharp nudge with your heels if he's trying to slow down. The more he stretches and marches forward, the more he will overtrack but this must not be muddled with just a fast, hurried walk where he will not be able to swing and open up his stride as much.

● He jogs during the walk or when the reins are gathered up after a free walk.
Solution Tension or anticipating the next movement can lead to a horse jogging. It is harder for him to jog if he is truly stretching. It's also tempting for a rider to 'back off' a tense horse. But try to keep your leg on (in a supporting way) and even ask for some leg-yield at walk to prevent him from jogging. If you sit too quietly on a tense horse with no leg on, when it comes to the next movement he is likely to over-react to any leg aid.

Give him a break to stretch his topline

How to create expression

Expanding the paces

- **Canter and counter-canter** • **'Forward and back'**
- **Medium strides** • **Pole work**

The aim

The canter is a three-beat gait followed by a suspension phase, when all four feet are off the ground (below). In the canter, a novice or young horse who is balanced will travel forward parallel with the ground, while an unbalanced horse will appear 'downhill', using his head and neck to balance himself – often seen by an exaggerated rocking movement. But an advanced horse will lower his hindquarters as he engages the hindleg and appear to travel 'uphill' (left).

Therefore, one of the key elements you should be striving for in your training sessions is the development of better balance in your horse. By teaching him to carry himself in 'self-carriage', whereby he shifts more of his weight from the forehand to the hindquarters, he becomes more balanced, more agile and more capable of being able to perform some of the more testing movements of dressage – of which counter-canter is one.

My way

Always reward your horse with your voice and a pat when he does things well. If, however, he makes a mistake – for example, by breaking into trot when you're trying to collect the canter – correct the mistake immediately and reward him when he does well. Repetition and being consistent with your corrections is how your horse will learn.

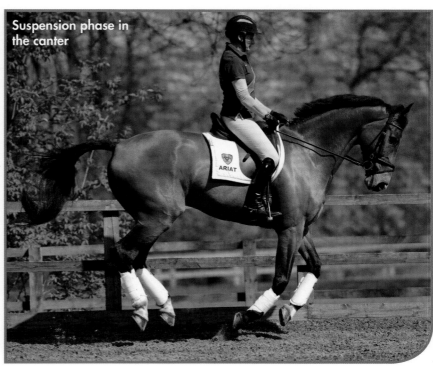

Suspension phase in the canter

Counter-canter

The counter-canter is more demanding than the 'true' canter which, for example, leads with the right leg when the horse is travelling right. But the counter-canter leads with the left leg when cantering to the right, with the horse staying flexed towards the left leg. Counter-canter should only be introduced once the horse's true canter is established, he is stronger in his frame and nicely balanced and supple.

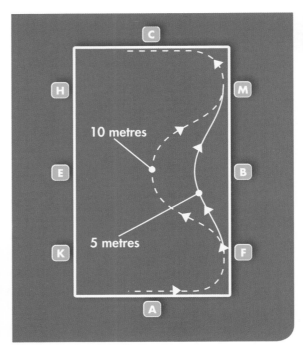

10 metres

5 metres

Give clear aids for the counter-canter

How to ride it

The rider

From A and on the left rein, maintain a 'position left' with your inside leg on the girth (nearest the centre of the arena) and outside leg behind the girth (nearest the fence line). To help your horse get the 'feel' for counter-canter, ride a 5-metre loop off the track down the long side of the arena (above). During the first half of the loop, he will be in true canter then in the second half, counter-canter. As his balance improves, gradually increase the size of the loop.

The horse

When your horse can perform a loop 10 metres in from the track, ride a three-loop serpentine with the middle loop in counter-canter, then progress to a four-loop serpentine. Horses can have a tendency to 'draw back' in the loop or they may end up 'running', feeling they need more speed to maintain the canter. So practise keeping the canter energised, forward and in the same tempo throughout or you'll lose valuable marks in the dressage test.

Common mistakes

Counter-canter

● There is too much bend in your horse's neck as he comes back to the track.

Solution Have control of your horse's shoulders with a contact on the outside rein. Sit square in the saddle – if you twist and turn too much and over-ride the movement by pulling back with the reins or being too strong in the hand, you lose control of your shoulders so will lose control of your horse's.

● Your horse has a tendency to break into trot before reaching the track.

Solution Are you asking for too steep an angle before your horse is ready? Be quick to pick up the same canter and repeat the exercise with a less demanding loop. Make sure, however, that you keep the energy levels up, otherwise the canter will become lethargic or unengaged.

● Your horse hollows or goes disunited before returning to the track.

Solution You are probably allowing the canter to become too big. Maintain an energetic, engaged canter, not allowing the stride to get too open. Have extra length bend to make it clear you want your horse to stay in that canter.

Forward and back creates expression

Forward and back

Transitions within the pace – 'forward and back' – both at trot and canter, will also help encourage engagement, elevation, manoeuvrability and expression (flamboyance). To achieve this in trot, ride a 20-metre circle in working trot, then ask your horse to collect his trot a little but keep the hindleg active. Then move forward into medium trot for half a circle, collect the trot for a few strides, then go forward to medium trot (below) and so on.

Do the same in working canter, asking him to step under and engage his hindlegs then condense his stride to come back to collected canter. Do this by drawing your upper body back and keeping your leg on. Although you're not changing down into a different gait, ride forward as you would into a true downward transition – say, from canter to trot and trot to walk. Then once your horse responds positively, move forward into a nice working canter again, before repeating the exercise.

Then progress the exercise by moving your horse into medium canter on the circle, bringing him back to a collected canter, then forward again to a medium canter. It's easier to try this first on a circle, then once your horse becomes established on a circle, go large around the arena and practise these forward and back transitions in trot and canter down the long sides of the arena.

For best results

● In the 'forward' transition, keep your horse on the bit and round enough in his outline that the stride gets bigger and more elevated, not faster. As he moves forward into the medium strides, gradually allow him to open up his frame to help him extend the stride.

As you come back to a collected stride, do not let him pull down on your hands. To avoid this, ride him forward but use subtle half-halts to keep him round in his outline, balanced and in self-carriage.

Helping engagement

As well as forward and back, another exercise to promote better engagement involves cantering a 20-metre circle, then gradually spiralling towards its centre (below). Make it smaller depending on the level your horse is working at, but don't make it an impossible task for him, especially if he's young. The aim is for the horse to step under with his inside hindleg enough to maintain the canter on a smaller circle, but if he doesn't engage the hindleg he'll break into trot when the circle gets small.

Ride the canter with plenty of energy and spiral the circle down until you feel that your horse is on the verge of breaking into trot. Ride just one or two circles to encourage him to really work, then reward him by spiralling out gradually onto a 20-metre circle, using your inside leg to push him out. Repeat this exercise up to four times depending on how he is coping. If he does break into trot, re-establish the canter immediately on a slightly larger circle before decreasing the size of the circle again.

If your horse falls out through the shoulder, make sure you help him turn by using your outside rein against his neck. Guard the outside shoulder with your outside aids and avoid making the circle smaller just by pulling with your inside rein. Also be aware of the length bend through your horse's body – the smaller the circle, the more of a curve he'll have through his body to be able to stay on the circumference of the circle.

Encourage him to step under

Guard the shoulder with the outside aids

For best results

- While canter is important for building strength and fitness, there won't be any horse who's completely level on both reins, so be aware of how your horse is feeling. In short, you have to be his physiotherapist, helping him develop parts of his body that are weaker so that he finds the work equally as comfortable on both reins.

Mix it up

Whether you're riding movements to help promote better engagement in your horse or exercises to expand the paces and develop expression, keep him guessing by mixing things up a bit to keep him alert, focused and on his toes.

For example, as you come out of a corner in canter, instead of riding him forward up the long side, then shortening his stride and collecting him before the next corner, ride him forward around the corner. Then as you come out of the corner, bring him back to a collected canter so that he doesn't anticipate his next move.

Obviously, if you ride medium canter around a corner, don't ride too deep into it as it would be difficult for him to maintain his balance.

Pole to pole

Horses with a shorter trot stride or who lack elevation in the trot may find it difficult to produce a good medium or extended trot. But work over trot poles can be beneficial, so gradually build up to five or six in a row over a number of days. And ride consistently to the centre of the poles.

- To help your horse open up his stride, gradually increase the distance between each pole to encourage him to step more forward.
- Trotting your horse through a line of poles raised up on small blocks can promote more elasticity and elevation. This exercise encourages a horse to really use his joints and gets the back swinging. And a horse with a more swinging trot will have a softer, more supple back.

My way

Training should be black or white so that your horse learns the difference between right and wrong. So be consistent – try not to ignore any mistakes sometimes but not at others. For example, if he doesn't respond to your leg aids, give him a quick flick with the schooling whip. Then when he does respond and go forward, give him a pat and/or some vocal encouragement.

Having said that, recognise when your horse finds something difficult – maybe he's tight in certain muscles, in which case it's up to you to help him by gradually working those muscles, encouraging them to stretch and strengthen.

Varied exercises – at home or while warming up at a competition – keep your horse focused

Learn to leg-yield

The aim

Lateral work is good for improving engagement in the horse, creating suppleness and developing elasticity. It requires the horse to learn to move away from the pressure of the leg, moving forwards and sideways at the same time, and is a requirement as he progresses up through the levels. It starts with leg-yield at Novice level, moving up to shoulder-in and travers at Intermediate level and half-pass at Advanced level.

Lateral work

- **Leg-yield** ● **Shoulder-in**
- **Travers** ● **Half-pass**

Leg-yield

This movement is ideal for preparing the horse for the more advanced lateral movements of shoulder-in, travers and half-pass. While it doesn't change the horse's balance as much as some of the other lateral movements such as shoulder-in and half-pass, it still needs to be taught in stages and literally just a few strides sideways is sufficient to begin with, gradually building up over a few days. And whenever your horse responds positively to what you're asking of him, reward him with a pat on the neck and some vocal encouragement.

However, achieving a small counter-bend – in leg-yield, that is away from the direction of travel and positioned over the outside front leg – requires the horse to be very balanced. Equally, though, this exercise actually helps achieve and improve that counter-balance.

Leg-yield also promotes straightness in the horse, which is particularly beneficial when you consider that horses naturally travel crooked. Straightness is essential for the horse to carry his weight equally on both sides – and leg-yield in the trot and canter can improve this.

How to ride it

The rider

Start this at walk. Turn down the centre line, walk straight for a few strides then leg-yield to the right. To do this, sit on your left (inside) seat bone, take your left leg behind the girth and apply a little pressure to push him sideways to the right. Position your right (outside) leg at the girth to keep him moving forward and to stop the hindlegs from leading the movement. The inside rein flexes him to the left (inside), the right (outside) rein controls the flexion. Keep your weight in the centre of the horse.

After a few strides, praise him, walk forward on a straight line, then ask again for leg-yield. Keep your horse's body parallel to the centre line and long side of the arena. Then reverse the aids to leg-yield to the left (main pic). Ensure he stays responsive to your inside leg to push him sideways. If he doesn't, don't be tempted to cross your inside hand over the withers to encourage the sideways flow, as this will only create a false neck bend. If needs be, give him the occasional sharp nudge so he respects your leg aid and reward him when he responds.

The horse

The horse moves forwards and sideways at the same time, slightly bent away from the direction of travel. His body should be straight but with a slight flexion at the poll, so slight you should only be able to see his left eye and nostril if travelling right (or his right eye and nostril if leg-yielding to the left). The inside front and inside hindlegs pass and cross in front of the outside legs.

Once the leg-yield is fluent on both reins in walk, do the same in trot. Then once he is established in the movement, trot down the centre line, leg-yield one way for a few strides, go straight for a few strides, then leg-yield the other way, forward a few strides straight and so on. Also, make sure your horse stays parallel to the centre line.

My way

I will also ride leg-yield in canter – it's quite a good 'freeing up' exercise and helps promote forwardness. I would start by asking for counter-bend at canter on a circle and on a straight line. Then once that is established, I would ask for leg-yield at canter. If, however, your horse tries to make a change of leg in the canter leg-yield, pick up normal canter, circle away, then ask again for the counter-bend and sideways movement.

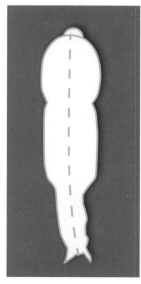

Leg-yield to the right

Common mistakes Leg-yield

● The angle of the movement is too steep and the horse reaches the track too quickly.
Solution Focus on the line you're taking and the marker you're aiming for. Don't forget that leg-yield is not just about travelling sideways but forwards too, so maintain the forward momentum keeping him in front of your leg.

● Too much bend to the inside, which causes the horse to fall out through the outside shoulder.
Solution This is caused by the horse backing off because he finds it difficult or the rider restricting him too much with the inside rein. Make sure you keep promoting the trot and check that you're not restricting the trot to achieve the required angle.

● The horse rushes and loses balance and rhythm.
Solution Use a half-halt to rebalance him back onto his hindquarters, to encourage him to push from the hind end rather than pull himself along by the forehand.

Shoulder-in

This is good for suppling, developing lateral bend, improving straightness and building expression by teaching the horse to flex and step under more with his inside hindleg. It's also the start of collection, requiring him to collect by shifting his weight back to his hindlegs, step through and under his body, lift himself laterally and lighten his forehand.

He must carry himself at an angle to the direction of travel, maintaining impulsion and straightness. But he's only able to do this if he can carry weight on his inside hindleg to support the movement, if he's free enough in the shoulder to stretch sideways and forwards and if he can create a length bend through his entire body, not just his neck.

Shoulder-in requires strength and confidence – how much you ask for and where you ask for it (along a fence or down the centre line) depends on your horse's experience. So if yours is a young or inexperienced horse, ask for just a few steps and build it up gradually.

I'll often teach my young horses to move away from the pressure of the leg out on a hack, using turn-on-the-forehand (where you move the horse's hindquarters around his front legs) and rein-back to open and close gates.

Leg-yield is also useful for walking a horse past a parked car or a spooky object – turn his head away from it, but still maintain the forward momentum.

When teaching your horse leg-yield, it's useful to carry a schooling whip to back up your leg aid and encourage the sideways movement if he ignores or backs off the aid.

Practise your lateral work on a hack

Shoulder-in in trot

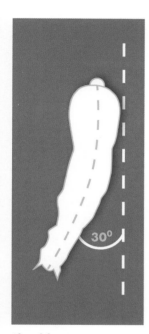

Shoulder-in

How to ride it

The rider

Shoulder-in should be started – and established in walk – before moving up to trot and canter. To ride the movement, on the long side bring the horse's forehand off the track to an angle of about 30 degrees, similar to the length bend you would have on a 10-metre circle. Control the degree of bend to the inside by keeping a contact on the outside rein. The inside rein should remain soft with a light contact and your inside leg should be positioned at the girth, maintaining impulsion and encouraging the forward and sideways movement.

Keep your outside leg behind the girth to control the hindquarters. Sit centrally in the saddle and look between your horse's ears, keeping your shoulder in line with your horse's shoulder. This position helps the rider's upper body to stay parallel to the horse's shoulders to maintain the angle. Some riders look to the end of the track, but this can cause the upper body to lose position and twist to become parallel – and this can lead to the horse losing the angle.

The horse

Shoulder-in involves the horse proceeding down a straight line, positioned on three tracks (outside hindleg, inside hindleg and outside front leg, inside front leg) with the inside hindleg staying on the track. He should be bent around the rider's inside leg with his shoulders slightly positioned onto an inside track and his body slightly bent away from the direction of travel.

To begin with, ride shoulder-in up the long side of the arena rather than down the centre line as it gives the horse the security of either the dressage boards or a fence line. Then when you feel your horse is comfortable and responding to the aids, ride shoulder-in down the centre line where there is no support – that will really show up how central his balance is.

Common mistakes Shoulder-in

● The angle of the shoulder-in is too shallow – for example, less than 30 degrees.
Solution Ride the occasional 10-metre circle as you proceed up a straight line, then a few strides of shoulder-in, then another 10-metre circle and so on. Then progress to moving forward on a straight line for five or six strides, then into shoulder-in for a few strides before straightening up again.

● The horse is not moving forward freely through his shoulders.
Solution This is probably caused by the horse being overbent to the inside and a strong contact on the inside rein. Keep a soft, elastic contact to the inside and try rising trot.

● You collapse through the inside hip when applying the inside leg.
Solution Sit centrally in the saddle with your weight evenly on both seat bones.

Bend him around your inside leg

Try travers

At home when I ride lateral movements in front of my training mirrors, I always try to achieve an angle/bend that's greater than is required in a dressage test. Then it should be easier for my horse to perform the movements correctly at a competition, when I'll ask for a little less bend. Remember, a horse will never offer you more if he's tense at a competition — you'll always get less, so that's why riding for more at home is really important.

Travers

Travers, which is also known as 'quarters-in', is effective for developing lateral suppleness and is often used to help improve lateral bend. It involves the horse moving on a straight line with the hindquarters positioned on an inner track. Travers, which is actually half-pass when ridden on the diagonal, is geared towards collection, whereby the horse must learn to bend around your inside leg. Often, however, young horses struggle with it as it involves engaging the inside hindleg more.

I'll start my young horses off down the long side of the school because the edge (or fence if you have one) helps guide them along a straight line. I'll begin with just a few strides in walk, gradually building up until they can maintain a line of travers down the long side of the arena. Then once they're confident and established doing this, I'll progress to riding the movement at trot and then down the centre line. This, however, requires accurate riding so that you don't end up drifting across the school.

Bring the quarters in on an inner track

How to ride it

The rider
Flex the horse's head and neck in the direction of travel, using the outside rein to control the bend. Keep your outside leg behind the girth to bring the hindquarters onto an inner track; your inside leg in the 'normal' position to guard the shoulder and encourage the hindleg to step under to engage the hind end. Move your weight slightly in the direction of travel, but do not hold him in position with a tight rein – ride with your seat and legs into a soft contact. When you've ridden a few steps of travers, bring the quarters in line with the shoulders then ride straight.

The horse
He moves on a straight line with his head and neck curved in the direction of travel. The front legs stay on the track and his hindlegs on an inside track, with his outside legs crossing over in front of the inside legs.

Common mistakes Travers

● The rider collapses their inside hip or goes crooked with their upper body.
Solution Your riding position will affect your horse's way of going. If you're sitting correctly in the saddle, then your horse has more chance of being in balance and moving forward freely.

● There is a lack of impulsion.
Solution Make sure the rhythm of the gait is not impaired once the travers begins. Maintain the impulsion by keeping him in front of your leg.

● Too much/too little angle is being produced.
Solution A horse will find one way easier than the other, therefore offer more angle. If he offers too much, ask for less; if not enough, gradually ask for more than is needed to help him stretch the tighter muscles which may be inhibiting him.

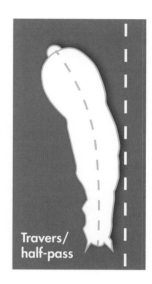

Travers/ half-pass

For best results

● With a young or inexperienced horse, first ride a circle in a corner of the arena, as this will help him maintain the bend and impulsion required for travers.
● Riding a half 10-metre circle from the centre line, returning to E or B will set your horse up nicely for a few strides of travers.
● Only ask for travers in trot and canter when your horse is established in it at walk.

Have a go at half-pass

Half-pass

Although the half-pass (travers ridden on the diagonal) doesn't occur until Advanced level, once your horse is established in leg-yield, shoulder-in and travers, you could try riding a few steps to test the boundaries. The aids for half-pass are the same as for travers and they must be very clear for the horse to understand.

Half-pass can be performed at walk, trot or canter, requiring good balance from the horse and effective aids from the rider. It is a pretty demanding movement due to the amount of engagement required from the hindquarters, but is good for developing balance, straightness and collection. What's more, it promotes suppleness evenly on both sides of the horse and is good for strengthening the inside hindleg.

Shoulders first

In going up a gear to trot, make sure that the rhythm of the trot doesn't change as you start your half-pass. So work on maintaining the impulsion you've created to ensure the half-pass stays forward and swinging. The shoulders should work equally as hard as the hindquarters, with the front end pulling forwards and sideways, the hindquarters pushing from behind. If the hindquarters get ahead of the shoulders – which can happen if the horse anticipates the movement – chances are you'll end up with a shorter, choppier trot stride. So to help prevent the horse from leading with his hindquarters, ride a few steps of shoulder-in before asking for the half-pass.

When you ride canter half-pass at Advanced level, it's often from a turn. For example, you may come from the corner to the centre line or from a half-circle back to the track. Once it is established, practise at home asking for extra bend in the head and neck, more curve through your horse's body and extra striding sideways to help him loosen up.

Common mistakes Half-pass

● The horse's footfalls become irregular and the horse loses impulsion.
Solution You might be asking for too much too soon if he's young or inexperienced. So start with a few steps and build up gradually, ensuring that he is sufficiently engaged to prevent him from falling out through the inside shoulder. Riding a few steps of shoulder-in before the half-pass should help.

● The angle of the horse's neck is bent too much.
Solution Remember to control the bend with the outside rein lying against his neck. This also helps the horse to balance.

● Not enough neck bend.
Solution Make sure he is truly bent around your inside leg, then encourage him to offer more bend. Once you have more bend, maintain it with your inside leg into the outside rein contact – not by pulling his head around with your inside hand.

The shoulders should lead in half-pass

Take a step
backwards

Riding rein-back

- **The aids** ● **Rider position**
- **Troubleshooting** ● **Improver exercises**

The aim

Rein-back is a great exercise for engaging the horse's hindquarters and lightening the forehand, improving the horse's balance as he shifts his weight from the front end to the hind end. Rein-back also helps achieve better collection, and encourages the horse to remain attentive and focused on the aids.

It involves the horse taking steps backwards in a straight line, moving his legs in diagonal pairs, and it is performed after a halt. As I've already mentioned in 'Lateral work', you can start teaching your horse the beginnings of a rein-back while you're out hacking, opening and closing gates.

When teaching rein-back to a young or inexperienced horse for the first time, initially aim for just one or two steps and build gradually up to five or six over a few days, concentrating on maintaining a steady rhythm. If he's tense or anxious about the movement and starts to rush, just halt and walk on before trying again.

It's important also never to pull the horse back with the reins – gentle squeezes on each rein is all that's required. And bear in mind that if your rein aids are too strong, this can encourage evasion and rushing.

How to ride it

The rider

When you practise rein-back in the arena, come into a square halt on the bit, with your hands closed on the reins. Then with your upper body slightly forward and both lower legs just behind the girth, apply a little leg pressure to create activity, keeping your hands closed on both reins – the horse will learn to use the energy you have created to go backwards. Be happy with one or two steps initially. Make sure, however, that you don't pull back on the reins – they are used simply to restrict any forward movement.

With your body forward, this lightens the weight in your seat and frees up the horse's back. This then enables him to stay flexible through the back and encourages him to take long steps backwards.

The horse

The rein-back is a two-beat movement, which should encourage the horse to lift and round his back as he steps backwards. The steps should be of an even length and regular tempo, and the horse should show no resistance when being asked to move backwards. In fact, he should accept the bit willingly, just as much as you would expect when asking him to move forwards.

As he steps back, his hindquarters should lower as he takes weight back from the forehand to the hindquarters, therefore encouraging the forehand to become lighter.

When first teaching a horse to rein-back, I use my voice as I do when showing a youngster rein-back from a gate, telling him to 'Come back'. I'll pat him as soon as he has stepped back for one or two strides, then I'll let him walk forward. I'll ask for more steps as he becomes established in the movement.

Do not pull back on the reins

Move your body slightly forward

Common mistakes

● The horse goes against the hand, drops his back and drags his feet, usually because the rider has used too much rein aid.
Solution Vibrate the reins gently with your fingers to encourage him to relax his jaw and come back into a soft contact.

● The horse goes crooked in the rein-back.
Solution The horse must step back straight, so you must correct any wobbles before they become a problem. If he continues to step back crooked on one side in particular, block that side by positioning him against a fence or the side of your arena to help him stay straight during the steps. And bend his head and neck that side before you ask him to step back.

● Do you find it difficult to rein-back?
Solution Get some help from someone on the ground. As you apply the correct aid, ask the person to push the horse back from the chest. Reward him as soon as he offers you a few strides.

If he resists, vibrate the reins gently

SHOWJUMPING

Gear up for success over coloured fences

Warming up at home

- **Hacking helps** ● **Varying the pace**
- **Begin with a cross-pole** ● **Warming down**

The aim

If you are riding at home and your horse has been stabled overnight, make sure you do a reasonable amount of loosening up before you start jumping. I like to go for a short hack first and then go into the arena and do my usual warm-up on the flat, as though I am going to do a dressage session.

Have the horse in a low and round outline so that he is working over his back. Trot and canter on each rein before you ask him to shorten through his body so that he is more together. Vary the pace so that you are asking for some forward strides that cover more ground along the long sides of the arena, followed by shortening on the short sides to make sure he is alert and in front of your leg.

Once you feel that your horse is nicely warmed up and relaxed through his body, you are ready to begin jumping.

Loosen him up before jumping

Imperial Cavalier on his way to third place at Badminton Horse Trials 2011

An energetic jumping canter

Allow him to relax and stretch

Warming up

1 Start with a cross-pole that has a placing pole 3 metres in front of it.

2 Begin by approaching the cross-pole in an energetic trot (rising) and with a soft rein, so that your horse can look where he is going and assess the question. Make a good turn and ensure your line is straight to the middle of the X.

3 If your horse lands and runs on, repeat the exercise in trot until he has settled down.

4 When you feel he is ready, progress to a small upright. Once again, a straight line is important here and the canter should be punchy and energetic. Ride around the arena in a consistent, forward rhythm before turning to the upright.

5 Jump the upright a couple times on both reins. Gradually increase its height according to the level you compete at and are comfortable with. There is no point in negotiating anything that is too big – you risk overfacing yourself and/or your horse – this is when accidents happen and confidence is lost.

6 Next build a small spread with the front pole slightly lower than the back rail (ascending oxer). After jumping it once, gradually increase its height and width, finishing with a square oxer (ie, both rails are the same height).

7 Your horse is now warmed up – his muscles are ready to work and he is focused on the job in hand.

I take my horse for a short hack before and after a schooling or jumping session

Warming down

Whenever I finish riding in my arena, I like to take my horse for a short hack to let him stretch and give his muscles time to recover. If the only option is to go straight back to the stable, I will finish my session with a few minutes of trotting then walking in a long and low outline on each rein. This helps him to unwind, particularly if he has worked hard doing some strenuous exercises. I always walk around until he has stopped puffing.

Perfect the canter

- **Preparation is key** • **Adopting the correct position**
- **Stirrup length** • **Jumping on grass and surfaces**

Good preparation encourages confidence

The aim

The rider's job is to prepare the horse as well as they can for the fence he has to jump so that when he arrives at it, he is in as good a position as possible to jump well. This will help him to stay confident and enjoying his work. Jobs to think about are...

- **Steering** Your horse must be on a correct line and you need to ride to the middle of the fence, keeping him straight in the process. Remember to land and ride away in a straight line – you must be disciplined in your riding at home.
- **Pace** Prepare the pace so that when you canter to a fence – or even trot – you are in a rhythm and there is plenty of power and impulsion in the stride.

All horses are different – some naturally offer a lot of energy that you need to contain and control so that you have a regular rhythm. Others are much quieter and calmer, which means the rider needs to create enough power and impulsion with their leg.

Bigger fences do not necessarily require more speed. This is an easy mistake to make, particularly if you are an inexperienced rider or you struggle with nerves. Bigger fences require a punchier canter with more power in each stride. As I explained on page 128, if you want a ball to go higher you bounce it stronger rather than faster in order to get it further off the ground. The same applies with horses. The more energy you have in the canter, the easier it is for him to do his job. He might still take off out of a sluggish canter with long, flat strides, but it will be more of an effort and the rider's job is to make it as easy as possible so that he enjoys it. Then he is more likely to want to keep jumping.

How are you sitting?

The general rule is that your showjumping seat should be slightly more upright than how you ride across country – being in a light seat is incorrect (pic 1). You should be sitting in the saddle with a slightly more forward pelvis (pic 2), so that your shoulders and upper body stay upright as you travel from fence to fence (pic 3). Hands should be soft in order to let the horse use his neck and body freely over a fence.

Watch and learn

You see many different styles in the showjumping arena. Some riders are more in the saddle than others and it is fascinating how quiet a professional rider can look to be sitting. Olympic showjumper Ben Maher, for example, is always quite upright between fences. He seems to do very little because he is not moving around and suddenly throwing his weight forward and then back, which would be off-putting to the horse. Trying to copy the style and technique of a rider you admire can be beneficial.

How often?

How often you jump at home depends on how much your horse has to learn. Young, spooky horses will become quieter if they jump two or three times a week. More laid-back/experienced types may only need to jump once a week.

Stirrup length

You should change the length of your stirrups between both jumping phases. After the showjumping, raise the leathers either one or two holes. You want to be out of the saddle between fences on the cross-country course, so your stirrups need to be shorter.

Ben Maher – quiet but effective riding

My way

On average, my younger horses jump two or three times a week, while the more experienced ones will jump once or twice.

Grids and jumping exercises are most beneficial when done two days in a row. This is because on the first day, the horse is learning how to do it and will probably make mistakes. It is better to do a short session and return to it the next day, rather than carrying on in the hope that the horse will get it. This means he could become bored and/or tired. The next day, he remembers the exercise and shows what he has learnt by being much more fluent and consistent.

Do not be tempted to jump too much. If you do two days in a row, leave it another four or five days before you jump again.

A lot of training is done on all-weather surfaces but you should also train on grass

Best of the ground

Most dressage and showjumping takes place in a grass arena at an event yet riders spend the majority of time jumping on a surface at home. I am aware of this and although I mainly use my arena, I will move fences out into the field as long as the ground conditions are good. This is particularly beneficial for youngsters and novices because they can feel totally different when there is a change in the footing. Personally, I always have my horses studded up when I jump on grass – even at home.

I find that while a horse is confident jumping in a nicely fenced-off all-weather arena, when they go out into a field they become quite green and spooky. When this happens, I step back a stage and add guide poles on skinnies until they are feeling confident – beware, though, because they can seem very narrow in the middle of a field and be spooky for horses and riders.

Most dressage and showjumping takes place on grass

EXERCISE 1
A line of poles

Pole work is vital

The aim

Pole work is an important part of every horse's education but particularly when they are young. Poles make horses think about where their feet are and they teach them to be neat with their foot work.

For best results

● The distance between trotting poles depends on the length of your horse's stride. As a guide, one decent human stride is a good starting point.
● Canter poles on the other hand should be placed approximately three human strides apart.
● Begin by trotting over one or two poles, focusing on keeping the rhythm consistent, a straight line and crossing over each one in the middle. Build up to a line of four or five in a row.

Play with poles

- **Maintain an even canter stride** ● **Poles on a circle**
- **Altering the stride** ● **Flying changes**

Young and inexperienced horses have to be taught to maintain an even stride to a fence. Do this by placing up to five canter poles on the ground in a row 3 metres apart. Start by insisting the horse canters quietly down the line of poles.

Add a small jump at the end of the line of canter poles, 3½ strides behind the final one. The idea is to maintain the same rhythm but some horses might spot the fence and try to rush. The poles encourage the horse to stay in a rhythm.

Canter quietly on the approach

Poles leading to a fence teach horses to approach in a regular rhythm and even canter stride

Only add the final fence when your horse is confident and capable

Exercise 1

77

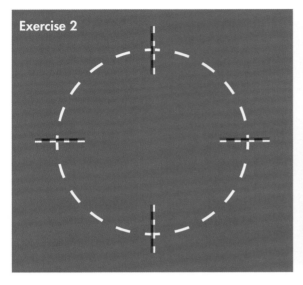

Exercise 2

As your horse progresses, ride a smaller circle which requires fewer steps

EXERCISE 2
Poles on a circle

Progress from a line of poles to four poles on a 20-metre circle with one pole at every quarter (see diagram, above). Start with one pole and then add in a second, third and fourth in stages as your horse grows in confidence.

This might seem like a basic exercise but it is surprisingly difficult to get it right. Stay in a rhythm which should not be affected by the poles – the circle should be smooth and consistent so that you meet each one in the middle.

EXERCISE 3
Altering the stride

Once the horse has got the idea of Exercise 2, ride on an outside line so that you fit in more strides between each pole while still riding a circle. After cracking this, you can ride a smaller circle and decrease the number of strides.

When you are doing this exercise, be very aware of the stride pattern and set yourself a number to achieve. For example, I may ask for four strides between two of the poles and then three between the next and so on.

For best results

● Make sure you do Exercises 2 and 3 on both reins. Your horse will probably be better at it one way than the other, which is something to be aware of but not worry about.

● These exercises make you effective as a rider because you become familiar with your horse's stride pattern and learn how to adapt it as you train your eye to see a distance.

● Horses also learn to listen to your aids and shorten and lengthen as necessary. It might seem difficult at first but practice makes perfect and it will become easier.

Canter poles on a 20-metre circle is a useful way to train yourself to see a distance

A single pole helps teach flying changes, as landing on the correct lead helps them to stay balanced when jumping a course

EXERCISE 4 **Flying changes**

Poles are useful for teaching horses to do flying changes. The thought of doing this can scare some riders, but it doesn't have to be complicated.

● Ride a figure of eight with a single pole at the centre. As you canter a circle on, say, the left rein, turn right as you cross the pole. Then the next time you meet the pole go left. As long as the canter has got energy and is engaged with the horse's hindleg under him, he will learn to change legs as you go over the pole because it is easier and more comfortable to do so.

● You can indicate which way you are going to go as he takes off. The following instructions apply when you are approaching the pole in left canter and want to land with the right leg leading in order to go the other way...

1 Have your inside (left) leg on the girth and your outside (right) leg behind the girth so that your horse's body curves left.

2 For the last stride or two, you want the horse to be absolutely straight.

3 As the horse takes off, change your leg aids by moving your right leg forward and your left leg back behind the girth. Open your right hand by taking the rein slightly away from the horse's

neck to indicate that you are going right.

4 If approaching on the right rein and wanting to land with the left leg leading, your aids should be adapted in the opposite way.

5 Horses lacking natural impulsion will benefit from using a small upright in place of the pole, because they spend more time in the air with a jump and therefore have more time to change legs.

6 This is a useful exercise to do with horses at any level because it makes it very obvious to the horse what he needs to do. Repeat it several times and be patient if he doesn't understand it straightaway. As soon as it clicks in his mind, give him a big pat so that he knows he has done it correctly.

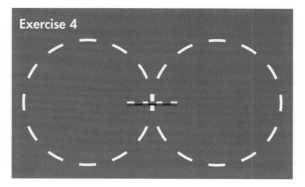

Exercise 4

Gridwork gives
horses confidence

Great gridwork

- **Creating an effective canter** ● **Correcting those mistakes**
- **Staying straight** ● **How to stop your horse rushing**

The key to gridwork is building a line of fences one at a time so that the horse has time to become familiar with the pattern. This will give him confidence and help him to learn. It means that you will need someone helping on the ground so that the fences can be added in stages.

The aim is to teach the horse to think about his legs and body and to gradually become more athletic.

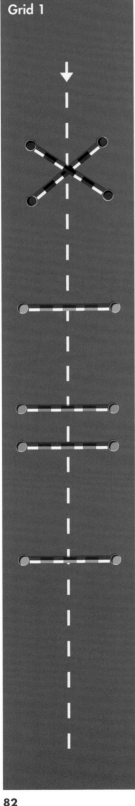

Grid 1

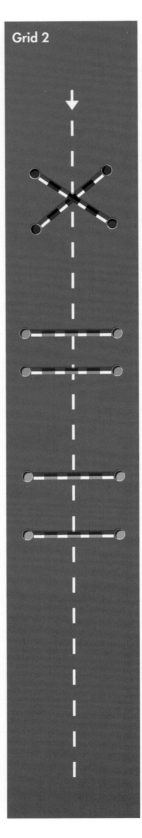

Grid 2

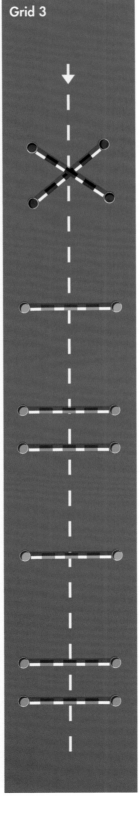

Grid 3

Progress slowly

A young horse might initially be spooked about jumping more than one fence in a row – be careful about the height of the fences so as not to overface him. Place poles on the ground first so that he has to cross over them, before gradually raising them into uprights. Then try the grids on the left, with the cross-pole being the first fence. Add one fence at a time and only progress to the next grid when your horse has mastered each confidently.

As the horse progresses, make each fence bigger so that he has to use his body more to jump. When horses are more experienced, it is a good opportunity to concentrate on your own position because there are no distractions. Think whether your upper body is too forward, if your lower leg slips back – both of these are very common – and consider where your hands are.

Canter correctly

It is your job to make sure that the canter you approach the grid in is forward and energetic. Then leave the horse alone as much as possible to jump with a soft rein. You need to be in the correct position so that you are not in the way – the quieter and softer you can be in the saddle, the less your horse has to worry about and the more he can concentrate on the job in hand.

Some riders are very active and hold their horse back before kicking forward for the last three strides. The poor horse must find this confusing and will be distracted by what is going on. Watch the professionals jump – they are so smooth and quiet that it looks like they aren't doing anything, even in front of a great big fence.

Create the canter and maintain it. Steer and then sit quietly but be ready to be effective and give your horse a nudge with your heels to drive him forward if you need to. If he starts to wobble, be quick to correct any crookedness and channel the energy forward.

V poles help a horse back off a fence

Common mistake

Too much speed

● The horse accelerates through the line of fences, which causes him to gain ground between each one and get closer and closer. After he has done it once or twice, the horse might settle down and work out that going faster makes the exercise more difficult. However, some horses need help to make it sink in.

Solution 1 Add a ground pole halfway between each fence (below). This gives the horse more to look at on the landing side of each jump and it helps him to keep the stride more under control. If he doesn't do this, he will probably tread on the pole. When the horse is running on, he tends to have his head high because the rider has a strong hold on the reins. The ground pole makes the horse lower his head and look while thinking about how he uses his body and legs.

Solution 2 Place the ends of two poles on the fence so that they form a V shape on the approach side (above). The V poles should touch at the top and rest in the middle of the fence. This is a good way to get a horse to back off because there is more for him to look at. But be careful, because he might find it spooky at first. Using V poles like this is also a good way to get a horse up into the air to make a better shape.

Add a ground pole halfway between each fence

Solution 3 If your horse is very keen, you could gradually add V poles on all four or five fences in the grid, plus ground poles in between each fence. This will really make him think about what he is doing. Once he understands what you want him to do, start to remove some of the Vs and ground poles until he can jump all the way through without any help.

Some horses may drift to one side on approach

Some horses push away from the ground unevenly

If you can, ask someone to video you jumping a grid. Then watch it back with a critical eye, possibly with someone more experienced. This is an easy way to improve your riding because you can see what you are doing wrong – it can actually be quite shocking to discover that your lower leg slips back or you tip too far forward too soon. Video analysis is a fantastic training tool.

Common mistake
Not staying straight

● Some horses may drift one way as they approach or take off. This will affect the distance between each fence because by coming off his line, the horse has increased the distance between the fence, therefore requiring bigger or extra steps to fill it. If you find that your horse is going crooked, you have to try to work out in your mind why it is happening. Possibly your horse is veering off in the last few strides of the approach or is staying straight until he takes off, when he pushes away from the ground with more power in one hindleg than the other.

It is important to take note of how your horse takes off and lands, so that you can prevent a small mistake becoming a major issue. Be consistent when you are training – it is too easy to let horses waver off their line on the landing side.

A guide pole will prevent crookedness

A pole on top of a wing stops horses drifting

Solution 1 If the horse starts to go crooked in the approach, lean one guide pole against the fence (ie, half a V). Instead of being in the middle of the fence it needs to be at the three-quarter point on the side towards which they are veering (above). Don't have the end of the pole that is on the ground too wide, as it needs to keep the horse straight all the way in. Alternatively, you can have a guide pole lying on the ground parallel to the line you are approaching on.

Solution 2 If the horse veers one way or the other while he is in the air, you need to use a guide pole on the take-off side of the fence. The best way to do this is to balance one end of the pole on top of a wing or in a cup on the top hole on the side towards which the horse drifts (above). The other end of the pole should be on the ground – it will look like half a cross-pole in front of the fence.

Guide poles help horses to stay straight

Common mistake Rushing

● Some horses naturally have a short stride because of the way they are built. These horses, plus those who tend to be stuffy to ride, might find distances long at a competition.

Solution 1 At home, it is a good idea to build fences on generous distances so that you are always encouraging your horse to open his body and stretch. If he is comfortable doing this on a regular basis, it won't come as a shock at an event.

Solution 2 If your horse is the opposite and he naturally moves with a longer, more open stride and gains ground through combinations, I would keep the distances slightly shorter at home. This gets him used to condensing and controlling the canter as he lands before he has to take off again.

Solution 3 Should the horse land more to one side, as well as using a pole as explained in Solution 2 (page 84), you should lie poles on the landing side parallel to the way you are travelling (above). Then when the horse lands it encourages him to stay in a straight line.

My way

Most horses need to do more practice with a shorter canter, and I find that I rarely build open distances at home. I spend most of my time condensing the canter and asking my horses to keep their bodies short in order to create an athletic jump.

As a horse progresses and completes more cross-country courses, where his stride will be very open, the jump will also become faster and more forward which is why I keep reminding them to shorten when I practise at home.

Imperial Cavalier jumping clear to help clinch team silver at the London 2012 Olympics

EXERCISE 1
Control your horse's stride

Play with the stride pattern between fences

The aim

This exercise helps the rider to become effective by being in control of the horse's stride pattern. It also teaches horses to shorten and lengthen their stride smoothly and obediently.

Essential exercises

- **Seeing a stride** • **Landing with the correct leg leading**
- **How to turn effectively** • **Teaching a horse to bascule**

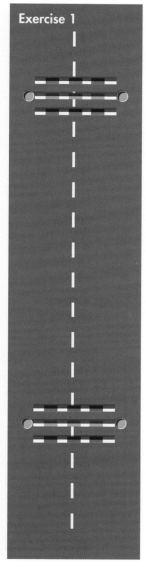

Exercise 1

How to ride it

- Build two verticals on a straight line, 24 metres apart.
- There should be 5 strides (24 human steps) between the jumps.
- Once your horse is jumping in a consistent, smooth rhythm and in a straight line so that he meets both fences in the middle, play with the distance by adding and removing strides.
- Count the strides as you land from the first fence until you take off for the second.
- Once you are fitting in five even strides, try to come in a canter that is more condensed. This makes the stride shorter and you should be able to fit in six before taking off for the second jump.
- When this feels smooth, you could shorten your horse even more and fit in seven strides.
- Commit to how many strides you will fit in before turning to the first fence.
- This exercise can be ridden on as few as four strides with an open pace or as many as seven in a very condensed canter.
- A horse who naturally canters with a more collected stride will find it easier to condense whereas a horse with a more open stride will struggle. Keep practising the exercise and it will become easier.

Common mistakes

- Sometimes when you start to condense, the horse might break into trot.
Solution If he does, turn off your line and pick up canter on a circle before blending back on to your line for the second fence.

- As you alter the stride pattern, the horse may resist by raising his head or shaking it. Then when you ask him to move forward, he might become excitable and awkward in the rein.
Solution The key to this exercise is to practise regularly. Before you start playing with the stride over fences, make sure you can condense and move forward quietly on the flat (see page 53) and then introduce jumps.

- Don't be tempted to just pull on the rein in order to shorten the stride, as this will cause the horse to hollow and raise his head or go against the hand.
Solution Keep your leg on so that his hindleg stays active and use your upper body, by bringing your shoulders back, to help control the stride. By doing this, the stride becomes condensed rather than losing all of its power. Above all, the rider needs to be effective so that the horse will listen to the aids and respond by shortening or lengthening in a smooth way.

Use your upper body, hand and seat for control

Commit to the number of strides you want before turning to a fence

EXERCISE 1 continued
Control your horse's stride

Seeing a stride comes with practice

Can you see a stride?

● Some people get hooked on trying to see a stride. At the lower levels, it isn't something that you need to worry about. It is good for the horse to think for himself and not always be presented on the exact stride for a perfect take-off point.

● If a horse backs off and slightly shortens or stands off a fence, he will be able to cope when you get it wrong. Every rider does at some stage – even if they are one of the best.

● Learning to shorten and lengthen is key to being able to ride to a fence well. It comes naturally to some people but for others, including myself, it can take years for the penny to drop.

● A horse's canter stride is approximately 4 metres long. On take-off, the worst you can be is either half a stride too close or half a stride too far from the fence. That is the equivalent of 2 metres to find by the canter being shortened or opened up on the approach.

● If you can go through the previous exercise (page 87) on four, five, six or seven strides, you are making a huge amount of difference to the ground your horse covers in each step – you are gaining or losing three whole strides.

● So if the worst you can be at a fence is half a stride out, this means you can do it. The amount of alteration you do is minimal – sometimes you just have to sit quietly – but if your eye is trained, then five or six strides away you can make a little adjustment to gain or lose ground coverage so that you meet the right spot for take-off.

Emily has a good eye for a stride but it took me a long time to learn

For best results

As you approach a fence, think...
● energy.
● rhythm.
● balance.

It is more important that the canter contains these three elements instead of you focusing on seeing a stride. When there is energy in the canter and your horse is slightly off in front of a fence, he has a pace that he can easily adapt in order to get out of trouble.

Don't do it!

Never kill the canter as you turn to a fence. Some riders only use their hand to collect, which results in a weak pace that does not have enough energy to jump. The rider usually realises this about three strides out and kicks on, causing the horse to run to the fence.

Where's the horse's hindleg?

When the horse's canter is condensed, the energy is suppressed. However, when it is slow and unenergetic, as soon as you ride forward, the horse's hindleg is further away, therefore limiting his ability to push up off the ground. He might still jump, but it will not be as easy to go up and over and so the horse will jump more forward.

If the rider has established an energetic canter with the horse's hindleg under him around the corner and all the way to the take-off, then the horse can really push up off the ground.

This is a prime example of how, often without realising it, riders make it more difficult for horses to do their job. The easier it is, the more they will enjoy jumping and want to do more for you in the future.

A condensed canter with suppressed energy

Imperial Cavalier jumping clear at Burghley and finishing third in 2008

Land with the correct leg leading

The figure of eight encourages you to think ahead to the next fence and keep riding forward. It is great for both horse and rider to help them learn what is a good, energetic jumping canter and how to keep it going in a balanced way, which can be surprisingly difficult to do.

Exercise 2

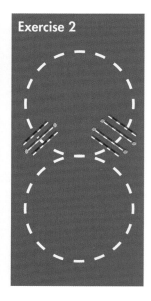

EXERCISE 2
Figure of eight

How to ride it

- Build two fences on a slight angle with them angled in towards the circle you will be riding.
- One fence should be a vertical and the other an oxer.
- Pick up an energetic canter that is travelling forward in an even rhythm.
- Turn to the vertical.
- As you take off, indicate to the horse which way you will be going on landing. For example, if you approached on the right rein, you will land and circle left, so look in that direction and change your leg aids as the horse is about to take off over the fence.
- As you approach on the right rein, your left leg should be behind the girth and your right leg on it. When the horse is about to take off, this changes so that the left leg is on the girth, your right leg behind it.
- Also open your inside rein by slightly taking your hand away from the horse's neck to indicate that this is the way you want him to go when he lands.
- These subtle aid changes give the horse every chance to land with the correct leg leading.
- Make sure you ride two circles as a figure of eight. Don't cut corners or go too wide.
- Continue around the circle to the oxer and maintain the forward energy in the canter.
- Again, as the horse takes off, change your leg aids to indicate that you want to turn the other way on landing.
- Repeat the exercise several times.
- Remember to do it in reverse as well so that you approach each fence off both reins.

After approaching on the right rein, open the inside hand (inset) to show a change in direction

Land and look ahead to where you are going

Aim for the centre of every fence

Common mistakes

- Horses who are new to the exercise might land with the wrong leg leading. **Solution** Be quick to do something about it. If the horse is trained to do flying changes, make the change in this way, otherwise return to trot briefly and quickly pick up canter again. Make it even clearer which way you want him to turn the next time you come around. Horses will land on the correct lead if you have communicated to them correctly because it helps them balance.

- The rider slows down in front of a fence in order to shorten the stride. **Solution** Look ahead to the fence and ride to the centre. Ride the turn well and keep the forward energy in the canter. The rhythm should be regular and smooth.

Land and turn effectively

The aim

This exercise is good for teaching horses and riders to land and turn, with the horse having to listen so that you can ride any way that you ask. He doesn't know which way you want to go until you land, similar to being on a course, and it is not the same every time he jumps through.

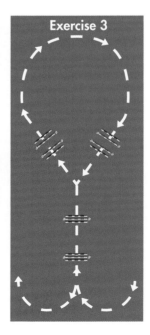

Exercise 3

EXERCISE 3
A fan for balance

Signal to the horse which way you will go on landing while he is in the air

Plan ahead and look where you're going

How to ride it

- Build two uprights (a double) on the centre line of your arena, one stride apart. Build an oxer angled to the left on a curving three-stride distance and another oxer or vertical in the same place but on the right (see diagram, below left). This means you have the choice of turning left or right after clearing the double.
- Approach the double in canter and off the left rein.
- On landing, continue on the left rein and curve around to the oxer on the left-hand side.
- Jump the double again, this time off the right rein, and curve around to jump the oxer on the right.
- Now approach the double on the left rein and curve right after clearing it to the right-hand oxer.
- Next time, jump the double off the right rein followed by the left-hand oxer.
- Link the exercise together by jumping the double and bearing left to the oxer on that side. Circle right to negotiate the other oxer back towards the double. Continue over the double.
- Repeat the above in the opposite direction. Once you have done this a few times and the horse has learnt how to do the exercise, you should feel confident that he is very in tune with what you are asking him to do. It teaches the rider to plan ahead, sit up on landing and look where they are going so that they get a good line while the horse learns to listen, respond and land with the correct leg leading to turn for the next fence. Using a combination of uprights and oxers means he has to use his body in different ways, which is good training.

EXERCISE 4
Brilliant bascule

Have the pole higher on the outside

The aim

Although this exercise only consists of one fence, it needs to be ridden on a 20-metre circle and built at an angle (below). Lie a pole on the ground followed by a small upright seven paces behind. Place another ground pole seven paces after it, all on a curve to suit the circle. The pole in the upright should be higher on the outside.

Experiment with your line

On each rein, play with the size of the circle so that you go from a tighter one requiring one stride before and after a smaller jump, to a larger one needing two strides before and after a bigger jump. Rather than changing the stride pattern, you are altering the line you take to increase and decrease the distance, therefore the number of strides. It helps familiarise the rider with the horse's ground coverage, teaches them to judge a distance in order to see a good take-off spot and maintain a regular rhythm.

The benefits

This exercise is effective for making the horse really use his body to jump on both reins – turning as he jumps, with a ground pole on both sides on the circumference of a circle. Both ground poles assist with maintaining the canter stride. If the pace becomes too quick, the horse will land further away from the fence but a landing pole helps to prevent this by getting him to look down and back off. This encourages him to bascule over the obstacle with his shoulders up and head down.

Exercise 3

A beautiful bascule

Approach...   ...jump...   ...and land on a circle

EXERCISE 5
Stay in control

The focus is on controlling the pace and staying on a straight line. The horse has to engage his hindleg in order to make the turns and not lose any power in the canter, so that he continues travelling forward to the next part.

How to do it

- This is a combination of fences built to make an X shape over X in the middle of an arena. Build two uprights adjacent to each other on one diagonal and another two adjacent to each other on the other diagonal.
- At the point where the two lines meet (ie, the middle of the X), place some blocks.
- Approach one jump in a straight line and ride away from it straight too. Loop to swing around

to the fence at the other end of the line.
- Do the two fences on the other line from the opposite rein.
- Now jump each arm of the X with small circles in between each. This means you will be approaching and landing straight from each of them.
- Jump over the blocks in the middle to finish.

My way

Be creative when you are training at home – I like to keep my horses interested by varying their work using different exercises.

It pays to practise

There are lots of exercises you can do at home, but do not forget that at an event you will need to negotiate a whole course. Therefore, it is a good idea to ride a course of fences at home so that you and your horse are used to going from fence to fence while maintaining a good canter.

● If you are fortunate to have enough showjumps at home, make the effort every now and then to build a complete course. Make sure there is plenty for the horse to look at, and be creative.

● If you do not have any proper fillers, you can make do with barrels or hanging rugs over poles – anything that can safely make the fences spooky and interesting. If your horse is used to jumping whatever he sees at home, bright, colourful fillers at a competition will not be a problem.

EXERCISE 6
Jump a course at home

I like to teach my horses to do a flying change rather than trotting to correct them for a turn. They will have started to learn how to correct themselves using a single pole (see page 79). Even if they are incorrect or disunite for a few strides, it is a step in the right direction.

How to do it

When designing a course, it needs to have...
- a variety of uprights and oxers.
- a combination, because you will find this sort of thing at every level.
- a related distance. This means there is a set four, five or six strides from one fence to the next and ensures that you practise riding a consistent stride.
- a narrow showjump, as occasionally course designers include one which can become a bogey fence if riders are not prepared. Some of my poles are 12ft long while others are 10ft. I also have a few that are 4ft, which means I can practise jumping a stile at home. If you can, it is a good idea to include one in your course, too.

Accuracy

Be strict with yourself and make sure you ride correct lines and jump the middle of each fence. As you come around the corners, do not allow the horse to fall in with his shoulder. It is tempting to let them get away with this but if you allow it at home, it will be even worse at a competition. Ride as correctly as you can and aim for perfection. If things start to go wrong, remember that you do not have to keep going. Consider riding a circle to regroup and get the horse together before you go any further.

This said, though, if you are approaching a fence and suddenly realise that you are on the wrong stride, sometimes you might turn away (as long as you have not got too close and consequently the horse has locked on), but do not make a habit of it. At a competition, circling or turning away will result in penalties so you must go with what you've got. Also bear in mind that turning away from a fence too often can be baffling for a horse after learning that running out is not acceptable.

Be creative with your training to keep you and your horse interested

Even my top horses jump courses at home

Your landing
matters as much
as your take-off

EXERCISE 7
Control the landing

The aim

How a horse lands and canters away from a fence is an important part of riding a course. If you are jumping single fences at home, it is not as important but when you are linking several together the horse needs to behave when he lands and stay in an even, energetic canter rather than running on and pulling on the rein. If my horse has a tendency to do this, there are a couple of things I do...

My way

As part of preparing for a first event, I would take my horse showjumping – either indoor jumping in the winter or to outdoor shows later in the year. Some regular showjumping competitions can be very beneficial to both your and your horse's confidence.

Beat the rush

- Practise landing in a regular rhythm by asking the horse to whoa and halt as soon as you can on the landing side of a fence. It must be done on a straight line.
- Keep pressure on the reins until he has halted and then relax the hands to reward him and give him a pat. That will tell him clearly what you are expecting from him.
- Continue riding a couple of strides and then pull up. If you are riding a course, you can ask the horse to stop after every fence.
- After a few times of halting, the horse will automatically stay in a steadier rhythm because he is expecting to halt. At this stage you can continue to the next jump without halting.
- Consider asking the horse to halt after every second or third fence, if he begins to rush again.
- Most horses learn quickly and this is a simple way to remind them that you are in charge and they need to stay in a good jumping rhythm.
- First, when I'm in my arena and they try to rush away from a fence, I sit up and bring my shoulders back, firmly holding both reins.
- If the horse is running through the bridle and not listening to me, I do the above and use the corners of the school to help me stop. Two sides of my arena are surrounded by hedges and if a horse is ignoring me as I ask him to whoa, I aim at the corner where the hedges meet. They soon learn...

If your horse is too keen, halt after a fence...

...and stand still on a straight line to make him listen

99

Consider the lines you will take

The aim

It isn't always possible to walk the showjumping course at one-day events because the allotted time slot is usually short and may clash with your dressage or riding another horse. However, if you get the chance, it is very beneficial to walk it.

From the moment you enter the arena on foot, consider the lines you will take. Which way is best to go on your horse? Is there anything that a young or spooky horse might look at? Which is the easiest way to get to the first fence? How many strides through the combinations and related distances?

Walking the course

- **Knowing your course** ● **Choosing a line**
- **How to work out a distance** ● **Watch others jump**

As well as walking a course and looking at it, it is good practice to turn away and run through it in your mind as well. Picture the turns as well as each fence without peaking.

The best line

Inspect each fence and work out the best line to approach each one. Also consider the best line to take to the next jump so that you are on target as soon as you land.

Stride out any related distances. You should be familiar with your horse's stride from jumping at home and know whether he is likely to run on and make up ground or need to be pushed on.

Preparation

Be ready to use your eye when riding a course and react to what the horse is doing beneath you. He may back off or have an awkward jump – anything like this will affect how he gets to the next obstacle.

As you walk the course, make a mental note of the turns and which fences are uprights and spreads or combinations.

Identify where the start and finish line is, too, as that is where you will be timed to and from. It would be awful to be eliminated for missing them.

Watch some other horses jump so that you can see how the distances are riding and identify any tricky turns. This can help you to feel a bit more prepared. Walking a course twice will ensure that it is really fixed in your mind.

The general rule for working out a distance is as follows...

- With your back against the first fence, step forward two paces. That is where the horse will land.
- From that point, every four steps that you take equals one horse's stride.
- Two steps in front of the next fence is the take-off spot.

Imperial Cavalier jumping clear for team gold at the World Equestrian Games, Kentucky 2010

Hone your warm-up routine

The aim

This is similar to how you should work in at home (see page 72), but you must bear in mind that there are other riders in the collecting ring with you and it will be busy. This makes things more difficult, especially if your horse is sharp, so make sure you keep an eye on what is happening around you. The general rule that riders follow is passing left to left – ie, your left side passes the other rider's left side. Be sensible – don't suddenly stop and never make a turn without checking it is clear to do so. It is rather like driving on a busy road.

Being aware of those around you will help to keep your horse confident. If you are not alert and you collide with another horse or have a near-miss, it can really scare horses and make them nervous about working with others.

Warming up at an event

- **Establish a warm-up routine** ● **Know your horse**
- **What not to do** ● **Enter the arena quickly**

My way

At a one-day event, my horse has already worked for the dressage phase so I go into the showjumping collecting ring when there are six horses to jump before it is my turn.

● I trot and canter on each rein before cantering to a cross-pole, then cantering to a small upright. After clearing a vertical once, I gradually increase its height. Make sure your helper is aware of any tape on the wings, though, as each height is marked and you mustn't jump bigger than your class.

● I finish with an oxer – small to start with, then I build up to one that is bigger and wider. At first, it should be slightly ascending with the front pole lower than the back one, but finish by jumping one that is square. This makes sure the horse is being quick and sharp with his front legs.

Relaxing in the warm-up ring

Above: Remember to put your number down on the board. Below: Most horses benefit from standing for a moment, taking in their surroundings

Know your horse

The showjumping collecting ring is usually quite buzzy, with plenty going on around the arena as well as inside it. If your horse is uneasy or excitable, allow enough time to warm up. I find that many horses benefit from doing some work and having a little jump before standing to watch a few in the arena, because it gives them a chance to take in the surroundings. Then I pick up the horse again and jump several more fences before going into the arena to do my round.

Calmer horses should get to the collecting ring and crack on. When you arrive, report to the steward straightaway. More often than not, a blackboard is used to display the running order and you can check to see if this phase is on time and how many numbers are left to go before you jump, so that you can judge when to start warming up. You don't want be ready too early, but you also don't want to be rushing so that you become flustered. I usually start to jump when there are five left to go before me.

The key goal for warming up is feeling confident

Get set – go!

When you finish your warm-up and there are still several horses to jump before you go into the arena, do not keep jumping. Stay walking on a contact – don't stand around dreaming – then when the one before you is about to jump, pick your horse up again. Possibly you will need one more jump, depending on how long you have been waiting, then get back to the arena entrance as quickly as you can so that you are ready to go.

The warm-up is all about preparing horses to jump – too much will have the opposite effect and if they become bored and flat, they are less likely to go clear. Generally, laid-back horses need to jump less than more excitable types. Build up the height quickly, providing they feel confident, and you may find that as few as five or six jumps is enough for them to feel ready to go. Sharper horses are likely to need a few more to help them settle. Emily's horse, Charlemagne, is nervous in busy collecting rings and she has to be very aware of what is going on around her and not expect other riders to get out way of her way. If other horses do get too close to 'Charlie' he can get scared.

As well as altering fences, it is useful to have someone on the ground who can check your girth and cast an eye over your tack just before you go in. They can also keep an eye on how many there are to go before you are due in the arena so that you can solely focus on warming up.

I help Emily and she helps me!

A fence down in the warm-up sharpens up a lazy horse

For best results

If your horse is quiet and lazy, work on getting the canter forward. Ride to the warm-up fences with plenty of energy and try to make him use his body. Don't worry if you have a fence down – it can actually sharpen a lazy horse.

It is natural to feel nervous or you may worry about it being a busy area or that people are watching. Take deep breaths and focus on keeping a cool head. Concentrate on riding correct lines, establishing a good positive canter and preparing for each jump – and make sure you ride away in a straight line, rather than landing in a heap and pulling up.

Horses who are careful need to be kept confident in the warm-up. Avoid putting too much pressure on them in the collecting ring – think about having several calm, quiet jumps, keeping them as confident as possible.

I have a tried and tested warm-up routine that I rely on, adapting it to suit horses according to how much work they need in order to prepare them to their full potential. As you get to know your horse and build a partnership, you can do this, too.

What not to do

I often see riders letting nerves get the better of them and riding erratically to fences. Alternatively, people get upset or cross easily and take it out on their parent, other half or helper because they are not coping with the worry. Be honest and ask yourself if you are one of these people. If so, being aware of it can help you to prevent it.

If your horse refuses or knocks a fence down, channel your nerves into thinking positively and ask yourself what went wrong. Most likely your line or canter could have been better or perhaps you were over-riding. Getting wound up won't help the situation and trying to take control of what is happening by working out why things are going wrong can help you feel less nervous.

Panicking and riding too fast is common, too, rather than concentrating on maintaining a rhythm and impulsion. I often see riders cutting corners or whizzing around too fast, causing the horse to lose balance. This is not setting him up to have a good jump, which is vital for keeping him confident.

On the other hand, some riders show nerves by riding 'backwards'. They have a tight contact and hold the horse all the way to the fence which totally kills the canter and can lead to a very uncomfortable cat leap. Holding the horse together like this is a hindrance rather than helpful because you are not allowing him to move with energy or use his whole body to jump. Having the handbrake and the accelerator on at the same time doesn't work well!

Be arena savvy

The quicker you enter the arena on your horse, the more time you have to trot around before the bell, which is useful for getting your horse used to the arena.

I think about the horse I will be riding and consider where I will go before I actually start my round. You are not allowed to show your horse a fence by riding up to it, but you can go past. Some events dress their fences and it is a lot for horses to take in so trot around and give him the opportunity to see some fences before you have to knuckle down and jump.

Listen for the bell as soon as you enter the arena because once you've heard it you have 45 seconds to cross the start line. Pick up canter that is forward and energetic straightaway – the pace you want the horse to maintain all the way to the end of the course.

Reward your horse after a successful round – and enjoy the moment!

Like mother, like daughter

CROSS-COUNTRY

Make sure you have everything in place for the ultimate challenge

Preparation is key

Getting started

- **Prepare thoroughly** ● **How to walk a course**
- **Picking direct lines** ● **Positive riding**

The aim

For me, riding across country is the real essence of event riding, when all the hours of schooling on the flat, the practice over homemade cross-country fences at home, the hacking to a friend's field for galloping work and interval training sessions, and accurate riding over testing showjump combinations come into play. All those hours of working to get my horses balanced, on the aids and working in harmony with their rider come together on the cross–country course – whether it be for a one-day event, a three-day competition or the Olympics.

It's probably fair to say that the cross-country phase is the most exciting for riders and spectators alike, requiring both horse and rider to be bold, clever, daring and at the peak of their fitness. But it's not just about going flat out to beat the clock, although speed is one of the requirements – it's also about jumping ability, confidence and trust, skill and stamina. In short, it's the ultimate challenge.

Vitally important also is the preparation at the competition itself, from the moment you arrive to the time you pack up and head for home – not least that first look at the cross-country course when you walk it for the first time. So remember that when walking a course, be aware of the line you plan to take, bearing in mind that you want to pick the quickest and most direct lines.

Plan your route

When walking the course, if you can, look back at the previous fence to check you have walked the most direct route and make a mental note of whether you need to be closer to a tree or another fixed object. Don't pick anything that is likely to move – such as a car.

Also make a note of any places where the ground needs avoiding – courses are very professional these days but not every inch will be foot perfect. Perhaps there are soft areas or parts where it is uneven or stony. Try to go around them or if that's not possible, steady your horse and hold him together with a supportive rein. Once you are through them, soften the rein again and move on.

On wet days, don't just gallop where everyone else has – look for opportunities to go to the side, which might not be possible if it's a narrow track. And if you're being competitive, galloping on the inside of where other riders have gone is beneficial because you are covering a shorter distance.

Make a note of any uneven parts of the course that need avoiding

Pick your line carefully

Be organised

If the event is close enough to where you live, why not consider walking the course the day before competition day, then on the day itself? That way it will give you the opportunity to make a note of which coloured markers apply to the fences for your class and to really imprint the course on your mind, as it's all too easy to take the wrong part of an alternative route if there's more than one class running that day.

When you get more experienced, walking a one-day event cross-country course once is normal, but when you gain experience and start CCIs (three-day events), you will have the opportunity to walk a course more often.

For best results

I'll walk the cross-country course...
- once for normal one-day events.
- twice for CCI*.
- two or three times for CCI**.
- three times for CCI***.
- four times for CCI****.

Forward = focused

Sometimes a steady clear round might seem a better bet, but actually horses are more likely to jump well if they have some speed because then they are committed, focused and positive. Therefore, always set off positively even if you are not aiming to achieve the optimum time. Attack the first fence and establish a good forward rhythm from the start, possibly with some wider lines.

Remember, however, that if your horse is inexperienced across country or if it's his first time out, taking the easiest route around the course and travelling at a steady, sensible speed will reap benefits. Therefore, always aim to complete your first-timer's first round in a positive but calm fashion – this approach will help your horse gain trust and confidence in his rider.

Set off positively

I ride better if I'm going for the time

My way

I find that I ride better if I'm being competitive and I'm going for the time because when I'm not, I then have the option to sit back and steady for a fence. And I believe that can cause some horses to think backwards.

Beware of going to the other extreme, however, and going so fast that you pick up time penalties for going too quickly. It is better to finish with a few time faults and a sound horse than winning on a horse who feels sore.

Speed is obviously a very important requirement of the cross-country phase, but it should be developed according to the horse's experience. And above all, it must be controlled otherwise it can work against you and become dangerous.

The need for speed

The aim

The more cross-country riding you do, the better judge you will become of your horse's speed for the level at which you're competing. Not only that but the more your horse competes across country, the more he should gradually become accustomed to what's being asked of him.

It's only natural for a young or inexperienced horse to get excited for the first few times out, but he must learn to settle, listen to you and respond to your aids. Don't forget that you are in the driving seat so it's up to you to control precisely how fast or how slowly he comes into a fence. And while you should obviously be aware of the time, galloping flat out towards a fence or expecting your horse to jump at a tricky angle could end in tears – with a refusal or worse still, a fall.

Learn to measure speed

- **Saving seconds** ● **Measure your horse's speed**
- **Learning from your mistakes** ● **Wearing a stopwatch**

Think forward

The optimum time is quick so you have to be efficient with your lines so that you don't waste any seconds. Remember, they all count. When you land, be quick to pick up speed and don't amble away. You must be thinking forward all the time so that you save every second you can. For a course of 25 fences, if you can save one second at every jump, you are travelling nearly half a minute quicker without riding any faster. And there's a simple way to measure your horse's speed...

- At home, measure and mark out a distance.
- Time how long it takes your horse to travel from one point to the other in a good, forward cross-country canter.
- Note the time then experiment with upping the speed and slowing it down.
- This gives you an approximate idea, but remember that it will take longer to gallop that distance when there are fences to jump.

Save a second at every jump

Beware!

Unless you are an experienced event rider and know when and how to use a stopwatch correctly, you could find yourself chasing the time instead of learning to pace yourself. Riding your horse around the cross-country course in a good steady rhythm and within his and your capabilities is far more important than speed.

Learning curve

There is nothing like learning from your mistakes. Sometimes horses are deceptively fast and course designers are clever. Also remember that different types of obstacles need more time than others. For example, technical questions require more setting up – the rider assumes a more upright position and condenses the canter to a short and bouncy stride, which wastes more time than a brush-type fence that you can gallop into and away from. Bear this in mind when walking the course and identify areas that will be slower and those that will be faster. If you progress to a three-day event, you will need to use the latter to make up time.

You can gallop into and away from a brush like this

Settle your horse before the start

The way to warm up

- **What to do in the warm-up area** ● **How to tackle fences**
- **Getting ready to start** ● **The first fence**

The aim

How you warm up is influenced by your horse's breeding and character, as well as what they may have already done at an event. At a one-day event, for example, they will have already completed a dressage test and showjumping round, unlike at a three-day event or hunter trial where you invariably have to get on him fresh, so need to do more work on the flat to begin with.

The warm-up is your sole opportunity to get the horse ready to accelerate out of the start box in a forward and positive frame of mind. If you have a horse who is naturally enthusiastic and confident, you may not need to do too much fast work. However, excitable types will benefit from steady trotting and cantering in order to help them settle and focus before negotiating the practice fences.

Think forward

When jumping the practice fences, insist that your horse 'draws forward' to each then speeds away on landing. If that means one sharp smack behind the saddle or a good kick, then do it – he must think and travel forward, but back up the reprimand with a pat or vocal encouragement when he responds.

Some horses may charge at practice fences and it feels horrible. In the past, I've had horses who've been strong and forward, and careful and spooky, but they usually settle once they get going. And spooky horses tend to become more positive the further they get.

However, if your horse is strong, try not to pull at his mouth too much – the more you pull, the stronger he'll get so ride in a relaxed way. As well as using your reins, use your seat and upper body to help control his stride.

Insist he speeds away on landing

113

Keep your horse relaxed before the start

Tackling warm-up fences

- Make sure you're positive when you start to jump, especially if your horse is likely to be spooky.
- Jump the fences on a straight line once or twice and if possible link a couple together.
- Next, approach on an angle and off both reins, making sure you aim for the centre and position the horse exactly where you want him to jump.
- If he stops, be quick to reprimand him – and even yourself. For example, were your legs on? Were you committed to the fence? Was the canter forward enough? Was your line right? If you can answer 'yes' to all of these questions, have a lead. Follow someone you have already seen jump the fence well to give you and your horse confidence. Pat him when he lands and come around to the fence again, this time by yourself.
- You don't need to jump too many fences before you start your round, especially if your showjumping round wasn't long ago.
- Concentrate on landing from each fence and riding away in a straight line, then continuing in a strong canter so that you establish a rhythm and good forward pace. Avoid pulling up too quickly.
- Remember, change the pace, particularly if your horse is sluggish. He will benefit from moving into a faster, more forward canter for a few strides before shortening again. Do the odd turn then go forward again. This helps get him in front of

your leg, switched on and listening to your aids.
- If your horse is fresh, the calmer you can be in the warm-up the better. It will help him settle and relax rather than becoming too excited.
- Be aware of where other riders are and what they are doing around you. The last thing you want to do is upset your horse or other people by cutting them up. It is dangerous and frightening.
- Always do a final tack check shortly before you are called to the start. In particular, check that the girth is tight and the saddle has not slipped back, that all the keepers in your bridle are secure and your horse's boots have not slipped.

Check your tack

King Solomon

Try to relax
at the start

Find a good
rhythm

The start

After they have been to a few events, some horses can be quite nervous at the start line because they know what's about to happen. If this is the case with your horse, it is important to give him more time in that area, even if it means just standing still on a relaxed rein or walking around quietly to desensitise him to the buzzy environment. By doing this, he is learning to relax. You can do this before you start to warm up or you could do some work and then stand for a while before picking him up for a final canter and jump before entering the start box. Always make sure you allow plenty of time – if you rush, you will get tense and it will rub off on your horse.

Some riders worry about going into the start box so try not to get tense. A common error is to tighten the reins because you are next to start. A clever horse will associate this with 'let's go', so focusing on deep breaths is an effective way of keeping calm. Walk through the start box two or three times before the final countdown and try to judge the final 10 seconds so that you go as soon as you get into the box, rather than having to stand still.

If your horse is nervous, have a helper on the ground – not necessarily holding him but quietly stroking his neck. Picking up some grass is a great distraction for a horse who gets very wound up – your helper could even have a few nuts in their pocket, but don't let your horse eat the grass or nuts just before he is about to exert himself.

First fence

The first fence sets you up for your round so make it a good one. A common mistake is to leave the start box too slowly and tootle along rather than cover the ground, which will result in an uncomfortable first jump – certainly not the confidence boost you need to help a combination get going. More often than not, it is because the rider is suffering with nerves so they ride in a restrictive way.

Imperial Cavalier – enthusiastic at
the first fence at Badminton

Leave the start box positively and find a good, forward rhythm straightaway. Horses are often quite spooky going into the first fence, so make sure you ride determinedly to it and be ready to drive with your legs. As soon as you land, press with your legs and ride forward so that your horse is thinking ahead and you're starting as you mean to go on. Keep your rein soft throughout.

Words of wisdom

Aim to maintain the determination you had at jumping the first fence for the rest of the course. Relax and concentrate to help keep your horse focused on the job in hand, maintaining a good forward canter and following the exact track you decided on when you walked the course. And never for a moment start to think that a course seems too simple.

As my heroine – event rider Sheila Willcox – says in her training book, 'The Event Horse': "Beware of the occasions when the course seems too simple. The danger then will be your lack of concentrated effort and the consequent possibility of an unnecessary mistake. The only easy courses are those you have jumped."

Great advice...

The aim

How you are sitting plays a big part in how your horse moves and performs. A good lower leg position is crucial because it anchors your whole body in the saddle. Every rider must be able to maintain a good lower leg position for an entire cross-country round.

CHATSWORTH
646

al bank

HSB
The world

Slip your reins at a drop

Are you sitting correctly?

- **Secure your lower leg** ● **Control your upper body**
- **Adapting to different fences** ● **Move away from a jump quickly**

Leg position

Your lower leg should be slightly forward, lying on the girth. If you position it slightly back, it is likely to lift up and swing back in the air when you jump. As soon as that happens, your heel comes up and you are very insecure in the saddle. Your upper body will probably tip forward and there's a high chance you will fall off if the horse hits the fence or pecks on landing. Even if he doesn't, it's not a great feeling for you or him and a confidence knock is difficult to overcome when you are riding in a competitive environment, particularly at an early fence.

If your lower leg stays in the right position, you shouldn't fall off – unless the horse falls over. You are also in a good position to respond quickly should your horse spook or back off in front of a fence. When this happens, there is nothing as effective as a good Pony Club kick to tell the horse to go. The most common mistake that I see is a horse spooking, the rider growling and thrusting with their seat, but doing nothing with their lower leg. That sends very confusing signals to the horse. Your balance needs to be secure enough that you can keep using your legs, but maintain a soft contact with the reins. This makes it very clear to the horse that you want him to go forward.

Correct – lower leg forward

Incorrect – lower leg back

Your upper body

While the position of your lower leg should never change, your upper body does. In-between fences, your bottom should be slightly out of the saddle and upper body slightly in front of the vertical. You should pivot in your ankles with your bottom lightly touching the saddle on each stride. This means you are close to the horse without being a heavy weight on his back. This is the most comfortable way for him to carry you because he can still use his back muscles rather than being restricted by a rider who is bouncing up and down.

In short, give your horse plenty of freedom so that he can think for himself, but be ready to act quickly and address any problems if something goes wrong. And be careful not to stand too high in the saddle, because this will make you insecure in your position.

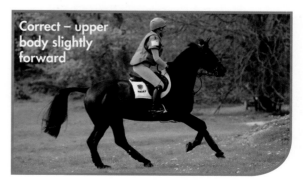

Correct – upper body slightly forward

Different fences

The type of fence dictates how you should be positioned on the approach. If it is some sort of brush fence or an ascending oxer, sit still and let the horse keep travelling forward to it. You are in charge of keeping the horse in the middle of the fence and more experienced riders will adjust the stride so that he gets to a good take-off spot. Try to do as little as possible.

Sit still and…

…do as little as possible

More technical obstacles, such as a rail-ditch-rail combination, require a condensed stride for which the horse will need to be slowed down and asked to shorten, so that his hindleg comes under. This sort of stride makes a horse more agile and athletic. You must, however, bring your shoulders back to indicate to the horse that he needs to slow down – and don't be afraid to use your voice. A lot of horses respond well to this and they have very astute hearing, so it only needs to be a soft 'whoa' or 'steady' to help him understand your aids.

Your hands should be slightly higher compared to when you're galloping on the flat – there is more contact to help your horse steady and taking your upper body back supports your hands. The more balanced you are, the better. That means you need to be fit and have good core strength, so that you are not flopping around on the horse's back. While professional riders make it look easy and are ready to act if they need to, some less experienced riders look awkward and appear to move a lot, especially if they are not fit enough.

Condense your horse's stride before a ditch

Move away quickly

As soon as you land from a fence, get back into the correct position immediately and gather up the reins, especially if you have had to slip them for a drop (below), so that you are supporting and directing the horse straightaway. Moving away quickly is also important for achieving the optimum time.

If your horse jumps a fence well, he will respond to a gentle pat, not a huge slap on his neck which is distracting. Remember, horses can feel a tiny fly land on their body, so be gentle.

Slip your reins for a drop

Imperial Cavalier – turning
with the outside rein

Common mistakes

● All too often I see some novice and inexperienced riders riding erratically and galloping up to a fence. They'll then invariably haul at the horse's mouth to slow the canter down at the last second.
Solution Changes in speed should be smooth and executed using your whole body. So start to sit up as you pick your line – with correct training your horse will listen and react by naturally steadying himself – then you have less to do in front of the fence and you can allow your horse to keep thinking and travelling forward.

● Pulling with one rein to make a turn, particularly on twisty courses is also a common sight.
Solution You should, however, be guiding the whole horse around the bend. This means that his outside shoulder needs to come around too, but this won't happen without support from the outside rein and leg. Therefore, open up the inside rein by bringing it away from the horse's neck and have the outside rein against the horse's neck (left). Use your outside leg to push him in the direction you want to go and have the inside leg on the girth to support that movement.

When it goes wrong

Not every cross-country round will go to plan. If I feel that something is going wrong – perhaps my horse feels off colour, is unwilling to go forward or he is starting to lose confidence – I'll pull him up and call it a day. There's no shame in doing that at any level. Don't risk having a fall or making a mistake because you carried on.

In the event of a run-out or a refusal, it is important not to give up immediately. However, if it feels as if your horse has given up or has lost all confidence, then it's best to retire and go back to basics with him at home. The horse's welfare is more important than anything, so never lose patience. If, however, you can quickly work out in front of the fence what went wrong and why – and you feel you can correct it – then try approaching the fence again.

Nerves are normal

If I'm riding a big strong horse and wondering whether I will be able to hold him as I warm up, nerves do kick in. Therefore, I say to myself that I don't have to do it and if things go wrong, I can easily pull up. That really gives me confidence. Some horse-and-rider combinations just don't work out – for example, I passed the ride of Chilli Morning to William Fox-Pitt in 2012 because the stallion was too strong for me and it would have been unfair to expect him to adapt his natural way of going to suit me. They have gone on to achieve great things together.

Cross-country is a mind game and your brain knows that it is dangerous, so a part of it is telling you not to do it. Override those negative thoughts and try to be positive by focusing on what you can do about it. I do quite a bit of visualisation leading up to a competition. If you get a chance to watch riders you admire, have that picture in your mind as it will help. That's how I learnt a huge amount of my cross-country riding by copying things that the likes of Lucinda Green and Mark Todd do. I imagine galloping brilliantly around the course and crossing the finish line clear and in the time!

Take advantage of
natural features

Dealing with ditches

- **Introducing ditches** ● **Clearing trakehners**
- **How to negotiate ditch combinations** ● **My experience**

Create a
pretend ditch

Prepare for him
to be spooky

The aim

It is possible to do a certain amount of preparation for jumping ditches at home. Therefore, be resourceful and create a pretend ditch using feed bags or tarpaulin – in fact, anything that you can lie on the ground and secure with poles so that it doesn't move is suitable. However, don't make the 'ditch' too wide – start with something narrow. Some horses take to jumping ditches easily while others may be spooky and petrified, so keep popping over them until your horse does them quietly and confidently.

Natural features

When starting my horses over ditches, I use a stream that snakes through a friendly farmer's field – it is narrow at one end, wider at another which makes it brilliant for jumping. Initially, I'll walk a young or inexperienced horse alongside the ditch and let him stretch down to sniff, then I'll turn towards it and ask him to jump it.

I'll approach in a strong, rhythmical trot, one with power but not speed so that I have time to react should he stop. If my horse skids to a halt in front of it, I'll encourage him to do it from a standstill because he must learn that turning around is not an option.

Encourage him to jump,
even from a standstill

For best results

- When I walk my horses alongside the stream and let them stretch down to look, I won't walk straight up to the ditch with the intention of stopping – that encourages horses to refuse.

  Also, once they are improving and becoming more confident over the ditch, I'll gradually back off and become less forceful in my riding. By the end of the session at the stream, I'll jump the wider part, approaching it in rising trot and on a loose rein so that my horse can look as they jump.

  A canter stride measures about 4 metres, so a 2 metre-wide ditch is easily within a horse's capabilities from a slower pace. And I know when my horse is happy because he will maintain a steady forward pace, even when my leg is soft and my rein is loose.

Start small, build up

Manmade ditches

I find that it's really beneficial to visit cross-country courses for schooling sessions prior to competing. Most places have several ditches of different sizes, so always start with the smallest and gradually build up. And if you have an uncomfortable jump, return to the smaller ditch. Above all, do everything you can to keep your horse confident and as he relaxes, think about slowing the speed. Come in at a steadier trot and a softer rein so that he jumps calmly with little encouragement. Remember, however, to have your leg there and

keep some power in the trot despite it being slow.

Some horses are naturally fearful of ditches – maybe they've had an accident earlier in their life, one too many bad jumps or they've never been taught how to jump them properly. Your job as teacher is to look after him, so only increase the difficulty of the ditch gradually – and remember, this applies to any type of fence. Never be tempted to jump the biggest one without doing the preparatory work, because one bad jump could put your horse off for life.

My way

I like to put over-reach boots on my young or inexperienced horses, just in case they are spooky and jump awkwardly which could cause them to catch themselves.

Also, if a young horse is worried about jumping a ditch or any other type of fence, it can help to give him a lead from a more experienced horse. And remember that a calm, quiet word helps some horses because it reassures them that you are there supporting them and that you are pleased with what they're doing – and that ultimately helps with your partnership.

My experience

Having produced a lot of horses to the top level, I have found that there is quite a big difference between the size of ditches at Novice level and those at Intermediate. I've had a number of horses who have just about coped with the width and depth at Novice level but once they stepped up to Intermediate, they felt frightened. In such cases, I take them schooling – probably a couple of times and to different courses so that they meet new ditches – to remind the horse how to negotiate the ditches, that they can do it and that they don't have to be frightened.

King William and Star Appeal were big, brave horses while King Solomon was naturally more cautious. As he went up the levels, he became 'ditchy' so I took him to Powderham Castle near Exeter – before Burghley in 2001 where I was

fourth – to jump some big, wide ditches. Therefore, even at the top level, recognising when to reinforce the basics is important.

That is why King Solomon didn't get to the top level until he was 12. At first, I questioned whether he would get to CCI**** level because he was so careful. On the other hand, King William was so brave that he competed at Badminton when he was eight. He won it a year later (1992) as a nine-year-old.

No two horses are the same and forming a relationship with them really helps when riding cross-country – some are nervous while others are bossy and strong willed. The cautious ones need to be given more time at each level so that they really trust you. It's easier to develop this trust with a braver horse as they want to do it anyway.

Big, brave King William

Trakehner

Trakehners

With a trakehner (a rail over a ditch), don't worry too much about seeing a stride as the ditch naturally makes horses back off. So keep the pace up on the approach, especially if your horse is a bit 'looky'. Have plenty of power and speed so that if your horse does back off, he has enough oomph to jump the fence when you respond with a firm kick to drive him forward. Bear in mind that the spookier the horse, the more speed, power and energy you need to have. This should not be confused with a mad gallop, though – it needs to be a forward, positive stride that is controlled.

Rails and ditches

At the lower levels, ditches in rail-ditch-rail combinations tend to be quite shallow and narrow in width, so they are rarely influential. However, as

Add a fence after the ditch

Add another fence

you go up through the levels, the ditches become wider and deeper, so make sure you practise them at home first using your homemade ditch (see page 121). Then when your horse is jumping the ditch confidently, you can add a fence one stride (8 metres) after it.

Once he is jumping it happily this way, jump it the other way – that is, the fence followed by the ditch. Then add another fence on the other side to make a rail-ditch-rail combination.

For best results

- When you and your horse are confident, you can vary the distance. If you are comfortable jumping this sort of combination on a two or one-stride distance, you should have no problem when you face it at a competition. It is also good practice to set the fences up as a bounce (3-4 metres apart).
- The same procedure should be used when negotiating a rail-ditch-rail combination while cross-country schooling. Always jump the ditch by itself to begin with, even if you do it at an angle so that you fit between the fences. Pop quietly over the ditch a few times until your horse is relaxed then include the rail. The final step is to jump all three elements together.

Ditch to a rail

How to ride it

Your horse needs to approach a rail-ditch-rail combination in a condensed, bouncy canter stride but be careful you don't kill the power in the canter by restricting the horse too much with your hand. If the canter lacks energy, he could run out of steam halfway through the combination.

As you jump the first rail, keep your body upright and your shoulders back. Some horses will land and spook then attempt to nip out to the side.

Others may try to stop at the fence when they spot the ditch behind it, or drop a hindleg in surprise, so you must be sitting securely. By keeping control of your upper body, you are in the strongest position to keep the horse straight and channel him forward using your legs. Lucinda Green describes it as squeezing toothpaste out of a tube. That is the same feeling you want to create when riding a horse through a combination.

When jumping a trakehner or riding through a rail-ditch-rail combination, I can't stress enough how important it is to keep your leg on and maintain that forward impulsion. This also applies to fences that have ditches in front of them, such as hedges and palisades.

Also, when approaching any kind of ditch, try to remain calm and relaxed. And these are good, positive, confident feelings you want to transmit to your horse because if he's relaxed through his body, he can make a wide distance easily. It's only when he's tense and tight that he'll find the jump more difficult.

Keep your shoulders back

The aim

A certain amount of work can be done at home to practise jumping banks and drops, depending on where you live. If you have woodland within hacking distance, use a bit of imagination to find small banks.

This helps a horse learn how to use his feet and body – it's surprising how difficult young horses find going up and down until they get used to it. Many will leap off the top but you want them to clamber up and down gently.

Begin approaching in walk and as with everything, keep the banks small and slowly increase the difficulty as the horse learns and becomes more confident.

Stay in balance

Banks and drops

- **Introducing banks and steps** • **Managing refusals**
- **Coping with staircases** • **How to jump a drop**

Trot on and...

...off the bank

Riding a bank

Schooling venues usually have a bank complex with different-sized steps. Trot on and off the bank so your horse gets used to being on top of it, then go up the smallest step before dropping off it. Give him clear instructions so that he knows what's right and what's wrong.

Approach a bank straight and in a good, strong, controlled trot and be aware of your position. Keep your leg on the girth channelling your horse forward then as he jumps down, allow it to swing forward with your heels down – never let it slip back or you'll become unbalanced. If you do get out of balance and land crooked or catch your horse in the mouth, it is off-putting and he may be reluctant next time. So have a soft rein so you can steer, but allow your horse to travel with a stretched neck so he can see what lies ahead of him.

When you land after a drop, continue in a straight line for several strides. The majority of horses naturally go left or right so insist that yours stays straight before you turn him. This will gradually become second nature to him and this is important because when you negotiate a course with a fence two strides after a bank, you won't want him to waver off his line.

If your horse is confident jumping banks, there's no need to keep schooling him over them unless you have a blip, move up a level or before your first competition of the season. The same applies if your horse has had a knock to his confidence.

Give clear instructions

Have a soft rein

Out of balance

What if he refuses?

The more banks you do prior to competing, the better. Increase the height when you are training, but always begin with the smallest at every session as it can take a while for horses to get used to jumping down. And be sure to approach a bank in a canter that is powerful enough to keep him going if he hesitates at the last moment.

The most common mistake a horse makes is jumping big and scaring himself, then it's a case of repeating the exercise until he learns to pop off the bank neatly. But if he stops, the bank should be small enough that you don't need to turn away and can insist he steps off from halt. It might take a few moments but when he does go forward, reward him with a pat and your voice so that it's obvious he has done what you were expecting.

127

Keep your horse straight in a sunken road

Sunken road

A sunken road involves jumping down a bank then up another one in quick succession with one or two strides at the bottom. And as you move up the levels, you may find a fence on the way in or out. Ride a sunken road as you would a bank (see page 127), sitting up in the saddle with your shoulders back and lower leg secure. A common mistake is to tip forward as your horse jumps down, but this puts you in a vulnerable position. And overfolding with your upper body makes it difficult for him to lift his front end when he tries to jump out.

Depending on the size of the drop, lean back with your arms forward as you slip the reins. This lets your horse stretch down and look where he's going. Then once in the sunken road, be quick to gather your reins without taking your eye off the exit. Horses must be straight for this – to reduce the risk of tripping – and have energy in the canter but not speed, so they can push off with their hindlegs.

Surviving staircases

Once your horse is established at banks out of trot, start cantering in preparation for a staircase – ie, two or three steps in a row. The canter needs to

have enough impulsion to keep the horse going all the way to the top. Speed won't help as it makes the canter flatter, then horses struggle to pick up for the second or third step.

Keep the bouncing ball in mind as you gallop towards a staircase in an open stride. Sit up and condense the energy in a bouncy stride – rather than slowing down – for your horse to make it to the top.

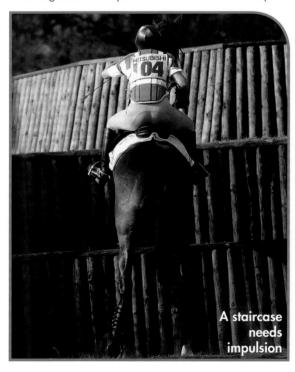

A staircase needs impulsion

My horse

My first ever team appearance was at the Punchestown Europeans in 1991, where Great Britain won gold. There was a sheer drop into a pond and I should have brought King William back to trot four or five strides out and encouraged him to stretch his neck and look so that he could work out what he needed to do.

However, the majority of horses I'd watched there had needed to keep the pace up so that when they hesitated, they still had enough energy to go. William was supremely brave and I made the mistake of cantering to the edge with a short rein and he didn't even see the drop. He cantered straight over the edge and fell on his tummy into the water.

My upper body is too far forward

Slip the reins to balance him

Tipping forward can lead to a fall

Jumping drops

When jumping down a staircase, it's important to keep your horse straight and in the middle of each step. Keep your shoulders back so that you don't collapse forward. You should be able to balance your body so that when your horse lands after one step, you are sitting ready to ride to the next. Your lower leg needs to be slightly forward with your hands relatively low.

The steeper the steps, the more you need to slip the reins so that your horse can use his head and neck for balance. Horses who stop at the top of a staircase usually have their heads up high so that they cannot see the fence. That is why it is so important to encourage them to stretch forward and down using a soft rein.

If things go wrong and you fall off, work out what happened. Maybe someone knowledgeable was watching and can help or if you're at a competition, ask the jump judge for their opinion. The usual cause of falling off when negotiating steps is due to your balance being incorrect with your upper body too far forward. If your reins are too short and your hands are tight, the horse will pull you forward. And if your lower leg is too far back, you're also likely to take a tumble.

There are many different reasons why it can go wrong so don't be afraid to ask. Working out what happened helps stop you becoming nervous about a certain fence type, otherwise it's likely to play on your mind and become a problem.

My way

If I'm jumping up two steps, I always imagine that there are three. If there are three steps, I ride as though there are four and so on. Aiming for an extra one step ensures that I am riding with enough power and impulsion to get to the top.

Teach him to trust you

The aim

A young horse naturally fears puddles because due to the position of the eyes on the side of his head, he finds it difficult to see directly beneath him – unless he lowers his head – and he has little perception of depth. To your horse, walking through that puddle may result in him disappearing down a deep hole. So it's understandable that his brain tells him not to go there.

To overcome this, teach him to trust you so that when he takes that leap of faith, he realises that he's not going to hurt himself. Begin by walking through shallow puddles – it is useful to hack out with an older horse who will happily plod through so that you can tuck in behind. Be prepared to spend time insisting that your horse steps into the puddle rather than around it. If you do this on a regular basis, he'll soon learn that puddles pose no problem and are safe.

Clearing water complexes

- **Make the most of puddles and streams** • **Schooling over water fences**
- **How to ride through water** • **Common mistakes**

Taking the plunge

Introducing a horse to water is all about taking things one step at a time so that he starts to realise that water is good fun. To acclimatise your horse to water, find a stream close to you with areas that are accessible to horses. Begin with an easy crossing and take an experienced horse with you so that your horse learns by example. It's important to avoid arguments with your horse because fighting with him won't achieve anything. Your aim is to make him be confident and believe in himself.

Have a long rein as your horse walks through the water to encourage him to stretch his neck down and look at it. Do not allow him to go dashing through with his head up – he will learn to be confident by looking down. Stop in a shallow place, then let him put his head down to sniff and play. Some horses might paw at the water which is good, but be careful that they don't enjoy it too much and try to roll!

Follow an experienced horse

Have a long rein to let him stretch

Help build his confidence

My way

The River Sid runs along the bottom of a valley close to where I live in Salcombe Regis, Devon, and there are places where I can walk the horses in safely. Then I'll ride up the river where I know the footing is good.

Horses cope better with first climbing up a bank out of water before stepping down into it. So I'll choose a small bank to go up then I'll turn around to go back in in exactly the same place. It's important to do this, because the horse is already familiar with the footing so should realise that he'll be safe. Some horses might hover then leap, so be prepared.

On the other hand, some will try to whip round but remember, turning around is not an option so do your best to stop this. And when your horse does go into the water, slip the rein to avoid catching him in the mouth and reward him with a pat and/or vocal encouragement.

Training your horse through water

Once your horse is confident in natural water such as a stream, it is time to visit a cross-country course to introduce him to manmade fences. It is rare to find a natural river on a course and besides, it's important to get him used to water complexes because they look very different, which can be unnerving for some horses.

Go with someone on a confident, experienced horse and follow them in and out of the water a few times before asking your horse to do it alone in walk and trot. Then try cantering through so that he gets used to the feel. There are usually slopes in and out of the water and if there's enough room, you could spend time circling and standing still so that your horse learns to relax rather than always looking for the exit.

Once your horse is confident, trot out of the water up a small step then add in a small fence a stride or so after. Then negotiate the step into the water, before next jumping a small fence on the approach. It is more difficult to do it this way, because the horse is so busy looking at the water that he may forget the fence is there and jump it awkwardly. This could result in him scaring himself and/or trying to stop. It's a big learning curve because the horse has to multitask with more than one fence to think about, but repeat the exercise several times and always end on a good note.

Just because your horse has coped well with water when you're schooling him doesn't mean to say he won't baulk when he meets a water jump on a course. Any new water fence is different so before your first event, it's worth finding two or three different water complexes to practise at to help increase your horse's confidence.

Walk him in and...

...let him look and sniff

Confident at walk? Try trot

Add a small fence on the way out

How to ride through water

When a horse jumps into water for the first time, he might misunderstand and expect to land on it rather than in it, so it may all come as a surprise to him. Equally, as he jumps out, the horse might judge the top of the water with the top of the bank. In this situation, all you can do is sit up with your shoulders back so that you are in a secure position. Then if your horse should stumble, you will not fall forward and get in the way as he tries to find his feet. Offer support with the rein, but do not restrict his head and neck movement by holding him too tight. Your legs must be on and saying 'go'.

As you jump into water, you should lean back with your lower leg forward. Slip the rein so that your horse can stretch his neck. Regain your position and gather the reins as quickly as you can on landing, so that you can guide him to the exit.

Defensive position on a young horse

Common mistakes

● If you go too fast and create a big splash, your horse will find it difficult to see where he's going.
Solution Make sure your horse has time to see the slope, step or fence coming out and register what he has to do.

● Your horse slows and tries to walk in the water.
Solution Teach your horse to trot and canter through water. It requires confidence and balance on the horse's part.

● Some riders find it unnerving to canter to a step out, wondering if the horse will read it correctly.
Solution Some horses will stumble, but they are quick learners so put in the practice.

● Some horses spook at shadows on the water.
Solution Be aware of how the sun will change from when you are walking the course to when you are riding. A dark spot at the entry of a water complex could cause horses to spook or they may misread a shady exit. A secure position and encouraging leg is imperative here.

Make sure your horse can see his way out

My horses

Imperial Cavalier At the 2011 Europeans in Luhmühlen, there was a hanging log into the water, followed by a fairly long stretch through a pond to a small area of grass with a large, narrow, box fence. 'Archie' locked on to the skinny on a forward stride. He was not reading it like I was and chipped in an extra stride. He caught the box with a front leg and we landed in a heap on the other side. Thankfully we were both unhurt.

Star Appeal The Trout Hatchery at Burghley cost me a win with 'Apple'. It was a step out of the water followed by a fallen tree on a one-stride distance. We came through the water and Apple misread the step. He took off a bit too far away and one front foot landed on top of the bank, while the other missed and he did the splits before stumbling forwards and unseating me.

Keep your
horse straight

Negotiating narrow fences

- **Practising 'skinnies' at home** ● **Dealing with run-outs and refusals**
- **When to use the whip** ● **How to ride a narrow fence**

The aim

There's a lot you can do at home to teach horses how to be confident about jumping narrow fences. Initially they will be spooky, even if the fence is small, because they know that there is the option of nipping out to the side. I think that slightly worries them because although they can see that it's possible, it goes against what they know is acceptable.

When teaching a young horse to jump a narrow fence, rather than just setting up a skinny, going for it and hoping for the best, it is important to introduce the horse to narrow fences gradually. To do this, simply decrease the width of a fence a little at a time. We use oil drums at home, first jumping two on their sides, then up-ending two together which makes the jump narrower and more testing.

I'd advise using guide poles to help keep a horse straight to a narrow fence – even if he has tackled skinnies before. Use them in the following way...

- Rest one pole on either side of a wider fence (above right) to channel the horse in towards it. Then make the fence narrower, but still with the guide poles at either side (right).
- Then when you've decreased the width of the fence and your horse feels confident jumping it, place the guide poles on the ground (below right). They'll still channel him in but more discreetly.
- Finally, take the guide poles away completely (see left).

Start with a wider fence

Make the fence narrower

Guide poles channel him in

My way

When I school at home, I don't always approach fences off a straight line. I begin jumping my horses at different angles quite early on in their careers, because it teaches them to stay on the line you've put them on. Even if the angle is acute – some are at the higher levels – the horse must not veer off. Despite approaching off an angle, I always focus on the part of the fence I want the horse to jump – usually the middle unless I'm aiming at an offset second element behind it – and insist that that is where he takes off and lands.

My way

When I'm riding towards a skinny fence, I imagine I'm cantering up a narrow corridor. I want to feel that the horse is between leg and hand, so that I know he is moving in a straight line. I am then more aware of any slight crookedness, so that I can correct it before it becomes a big drift and results in a run-out.

I'll always carry a whip when I'm jumping because it's a very important back-up to the leg aids. As you approach a fence, consider which way your horse is likely to run out – which he might do if he sees the stables, the exit, the warm-up arena or other horses. Have your whip ready on that side so that if he does glance off, your whip is in the correct hand and you can be quick to pull up, smack him on the shoulder and growl.

Don't jump too near the end of the fence

Carry your whip on the 'run-out' side

Run-outs

If your horse runs out, it's imperative that you are firm with him – he must understand that this is not acceptable. I see so many run-outs but without the rider reprimanding their horse. Instead, they'll carry on circling back around again which will encourage the horse to do the same thing again, because he has learnt that he can run out.

The first thing to do after a run-out is to stop straightaway – be firm with your reins to bring your horse to a halt. If, for example, he runs out to the right, reprimand him by giving him a firm smack with the whip on the right shoulder. Tell him off with your voice (I growl!), then turn back left towards the fence. If he has run out to the left, use the whip on the left shoulder.

As soon as you have turned back towards the way he ran out, you must then be cool and calm because you have finished telling him off. Try not to get flustered or nag because the moment has passed and you will upset him.

Allow plenty of space to pick up canter and turn back to the fence on a clear, straight line. This time ride more purposefully a few strides away, give him a little tap with your whip on his shoulder – the side on which he ran out – to remind him that that door is closed and he's not to do it again.

Right vs wrong

When your horse has cleared the fence, reward him with a pat and your voice to tell him he's been good. This makes knowing what is right and wrong as clear as black and white.

Horses are like children in that they will test the boundaries, so it's up to the rider to teach what is right and wrong – there can be no grey areas. Do not let your horse get away with something one day then pick him up on the same thing the next – that's confusing and prevents him from learning.

How to ride it

To ride a small skinny, approach it in trot, particularly if your horse struggles to really sit back on his hocks and shorten the canter. You will have more control over the trot because the strides are smaller.

When you start cantering to a narrow fence, slow and bouncy is crucial. This is because the shorter the stride, the more control you have and the deeper the point of take-off will be. If you see a long stride, there is more opportunity for your horse to jump out to the side.

Del Piero II and Emily confidently keep straight

● I always have a narrow fence set up at home and by jumping it regularly, my horses soon become familiar with skinnies. They also help riders feel confident. Whether it's an advanced horse or a novice, skinnies are a vital part of their routine.

● It's one thing jumping narrow fences in an arena, but out in the field they look very small and uninviting. It's funny how even experienced horses can be spooked by this. So practise them in a field – with guide poles if needs be.

● When the ground is good, I set up wooden palettes in the field, stud the horses up and jump over three or four several times, so that it becomes easy for them. Then when I go to a competition, I'm well prepared.

Refusals

If your horse refuses, use the whip to give him a good sharp smack behind the saddle so that he knows immediately that what he has done is not acceptable. Growl and turn away from the fence but then be cool and calm. Do not be tempted to keep nagging at the horse with your spur or yanking at the rein because you are cross. Also, do not be in a hurry to turn around and go again.

So often I see riders return to the fence too quickly and consequently have another stop.

Go well away from the fence, pick up a good canter and turn onto a straight line well before the fence so that you have plenty of strides to assess how your horse feels. If he backs off, be ready to growl, kick, use the whip behind the saddle and keep your leg on all the way to the fence. A kick with both legs is most effective – but hard to do! Remember, keep the rein soft. Once he has jumped, give him a pat so that it's obvious he has done the right thing.

Ride a corner
like a parallel

Coping with corners

- **How to approach corners** • **Choosing your line**
- **Correcting mistakes** • **Building a corner at home**

The aim

At the lower levels, corners have fairly small angles so you can treat these fences as if they were parallels. As with narrow fences, have your whip on the side of the narrowest part of the corner because that is the most likely direction for a horse to run out. And it doesn't matter if it's a BE100 track or an advanced course, I swap my whip several times when I'm riding across country so that I'm always prepared for the fence ahead.

Choosing your line

The wider the angle on a corner, the more you have to ride the front part of the fence at an angle. In this case, I imagine a line from the narrow side of the corner to the wide side, straight through the middle. I focus on that imaginary line as the fence – a parallel – then that is what I aim to jump.

This is where walking the course properly is so important. Spend time working out your line exactly, so that you are clear where the best point is to jump the corner. Approach in an energetic canter that is controlled but still travelling forward. It is easy to be so careful that you end up restricting the horse too much, rather than allowing him to keep going forward and be able to jump.

Imagine a line from one side to the next

Common mistake

- The danger with an open corner such as this one I'm jumping below left is that you can become overly ambitious. If you widen the poles too much, your horse can misjudge the question and try to bounce it – ie, jump in-between each pole if you come on a bad line.
Solution To avoid this, add a filler or lie a pole over the top of the two poles to partly fill the gap.

My horse

King William once had to jump two very wide, open corners at Badminton. Their narrowest points were on the left side. In preparation, I had changed my whip into my left hand. As we closed in, a plastic bag full of air blew out of the crowd on my right.

William had seen the bag and I couldn't afford for him to drift left, so I gave him a small tap on his shoulder to remind him to stay straight. He ended up jumping the bag as it crossed our track about three strides in front of the first corner. But he was a very good boy, staying straight and still clearing both corners. But if he'd been allowed to get even slightly crooked, it could have spoilt our line and possibly caused us to pick up penalties.

Approach in an energetic canter

Build a corner at home

Corners are all about practice and with a bit of imagination, you can build your own at home. I use two tall uprights, two oil drums and two poles. Then I put a ground pole on each side so that I can jump it both ways. Start with a narrow corner then as you widen the angle, jump the fence nearer the pointed end. Swap the tall uprights at the pointed end for blocks, a barrel or short uprights (left) and gradually ask more of your horse.

EXERCISE 1
Jumping an offset double

Practise angles and curves

If your horse becomes used to jumping acute lines on a regular basis, you should have no problem turning from one fence to another when you're competing.

EXERCISE 1
Offset double

This double is often found on cross-country courses, including at the lower levels, and can be practised at home.
● Build one upright at the side of your arena, with room to pass it.
● Allow a two- or three-stride distance then build a second upright, with its right wing lining up with the left wing of the first fence.
● Approach the first upright in a condensed canter off the right rein. Look for the centre of the second upright in order to make an accurate turn. Your horse will meet it at an angle, so that he is straight for the second fence.
● Jump the double in the other direction, too.

Exercise 1

Offset combinations

- **Jumping an offset double** ● **Riding a curve**
- **Approaching at an angle** ● **The last fence**

EXERCISE 2

Riding a curve

Build a treble – an upright, oxer, upright – each with one stride in between.

Diagram 1 Approach the first upright off the left rein, jump it in the centre and at an angle. Then curve around the oxer and jump the second upright, in the centre and at an angle.

Diagram 2 (pics right) Next, approach the first upright off the left rein, jumping it in the centre of the fence and at an angle.

● On landing, curve right around the oxer and jump the other upright. Turn back to the upright and jump the centre of the fence at an angle.

Diagram 3 When you feel ready, canter to the oxer at an angle and jump it across the centre.

● Land and circle around the upright, returning to jump the oxer off the other rein. Land and circle around the other upright back to the oxer. To finish, jump through the treble, staying on a straight line, in an even rhythm and in the centre.

Shorter sessions more often are more effective than jumping over and over again. Avoid pulling the horse around the turns using a strong inside rein – it should 'ask' for the turn. The outside rein should lie against the neck, to prevent the head and neck from having too much inside bend. If this happens, he'll fall out through his shoulder and become unbalanced as you are only turning the front of the horse, instead of all of him.

For best results

● Cross-country riding is all about smooth signals, forwardness and soft hands so that the horse can focus on the fence ahead. If the rider is sitting quietly, it allows the horse to think about what he is doing. The rider's job is to steer, so that the horse meets each fence on the best line and indicate the most appropriate speed.

If you watch someone like Michael Jung ride,

he makes turns look smooth because he is quietly using his aids to turn the whole horse. In fact, his whole round resembles a train gliding along a railway track. The horse draws forward to every fence rather than slowing down, yet the canter changes enough to be short and powerful enough to jump. Therefore, avoiding abrupt aids and sudden changes of pace saves time and gives both horse and rider a good feeling.

Angle the first upright…

…go around the oxer…

…angle the second upright

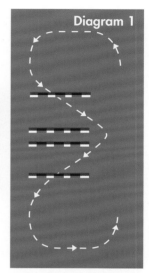

Diagram 1

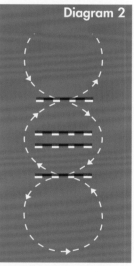

Diagram 2

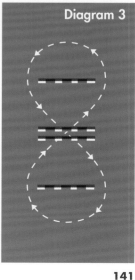

Diagram 3

EXERCISE 3
Approaching at an angle

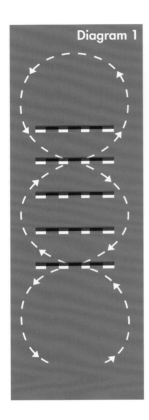
Diagram 1

Ride at an angle...

Jump at an angle

Depending on the length of the arena or field you're working in, build a line of up to five small uprights with one stride between each fence.

Diagram 1 From the left rein, canter to the centre of the first upright but at an angle so that you can curve around the second and third uprights.

- Swing right-handed to the fourth upright, again meeting it in the centre and at an angle. Then curve to the left on landing after the last upright.
- Continue on the left circle back to what is now the second fence and jump it in the centre but at an angle. Curve right, going around the third and fourth uprights, jumping the fifth upright at an angle.

Diagram 2 When you can ride this exercise smoothly, increase the number of uprights that you jump until you only miss out one fence each time you curve to the next, instead of two.

- Finish off by jumping straight down the line of fences, focusing on being in the centre and the horse staying straight. You may find that some crookedness creeps in after jumping angles which you must be quick to correct.

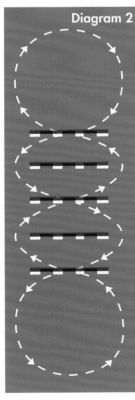
Diagram 2

...staying in the centre of the fence

Jump straight down the line

Good steering means the horse can meet the fence on the best line

Common mistake

● Horses who are young, inexperienced or new to the exercise may try to nip out to the side of the jump when you angle it.

Solution This is not allowed, so you should be aware of which hand you have your whip in as you approach the first fence. If, for example, you jump across the fence to the right, have your whip in this hand because this is the open side of the obstacle and therefore the way he is most likely to run. If you feel him drift on the approach, be ready to give him a little smack on the shoulder to say, 'No, that door is closed' and straighten him up. As soon as you have cleared the fence, pat him to reward him and quickly change the whip into your other hand so that you are ready for the next fence.

When your horse is more established and you are confident that he will stay on his line, there is less need to worry about changing your whip every time. However, if you are trying a new angle or adding a filler, you should consider which way he is most likely to try to escape so that you are ready.

The last fence

If something goes wrong at the final fence, it is usually because the horse is tired and the rider has not done enough to set him up for it – perhaps the rider is not focusing as much as they should because they know the end is in sight. Bear in mind that horses feel very different at the end of a course compared to the start, especially if it is an undulating track or it's early in the season and they have not yet reached peak fitness. Consequently, they need extra support over the last few obstacles – remember that you are not home until you have crossed the finish line.

Keep focused to the end

There is no better feeling than crossing the finish line, knowing that you and your horse have completed the best round you could. Enjoy the moment, but remember that your horse is tired. He may still feel full of running, but inside he is ready for a rest.

So often riders pull up abruptly or drop their reins, but you must remember to keep your horse together. He could easily stumble if you don't support him in this way and incur an over-reach injury or something equally silly.

Watch riders who finish at Badminton. They'll slow the canter before coming back to trot and circling – they never suddenly walk or jump off. So whether you've finished a BE90 or an advanced track, do the same, maintaining a contact and keeping your circles big. When you walk, gradually lengthen the rein and give him a pat.

Post cross-country

- **How to pull up** ● **Washing him off**
- **When to offer food and water** ● **The next day**

Washing a hot horse

If it's a warm day, water should be splashed onto a hot, puffing horse as quickly as possible. This is a key job for your helper and one of the main reasons it is really useful to have someone on the ground. As soon as the horse's body temperature comes down, the more comfortable he will be and the less tired he will be later.

Ideally, one person should wash down each side of the horse, holding the bucket rather than walking back and forth to it, while another scrapes the water off. Start at the top of the horse's neck and work your way along his body. Use plenty of water and splash it on rather than being too specific. Bear in mind that the water will heat up quickly, so you don't want this sitting on your horse. Allow it a moment to cool the horse's skin, then scrape it off and put more on. Repeat until he has recovered.

Splash water on then. . .

. . .scrape it off

Once recovered, allow him to graze

Keep moving

While washing your horse, check to see if his sides are moving and his nostrils are flaring. Initially, if he is very hot and puffing, walk him in a circle as you wash. Keep doing this until he has recovered, then tie him up and give him a haynet because he will be ready to eat. Alternatively, allow him to graze because this encourages him to lower his head and his nasal passages to clear.

At this point, horses will be relaxed enough to be rubbed down and have their legs washed. I always have old towels on the lorry which are useful for drying their ears, heads and legs. If it's a cool day, towel-dry him to avoid him catching a chill.

If my horse is cooling fast but still a bit wet, I put on a Bucas Shamrock Power rug to wick moisture away and ensure he dries. This is also the time to take out studs and plug the holes. And remember, most owners love to get involved so let them help, even if it's to hand graze their horse.

My lorry. . .

. . .has one end allocated to horses being washed down so that the other end stays dry. Then we don't spend the rest of the day trying to avoid wet muddy patches. Little things like this make life easier, especially if I'm riding several horses at the same event.

Lacombe et al (2004). Barnes et al (1995)

For best results

- When your horse is dry and happy, put him back into the lorry and give him a hard feed – he is ready to take in concentrates about an hour or so after a cross-country round, as advised by my sponsor, Baileys Horse Feeds.

  They say: "Feeding after cross-country helps replenish glucose and carbohydrate levels (energy reserves). And if your horse has not readily taken in electrolytes via water, it's a means of getting these into him.

  "It can take 48-72 hours post-exercise to restore energy levels to those pre-exercise, when using traditional feeding methods. However, research* has shown that higher muscle glycogen stores were seen 1-4 hours post cross-country when feeding concentrate and hay than with hay alone."

Leg care

There are lots of cooling products that can be applied to legs to help horses recover after strenuous work. However, they can be so effective at doing their job, it's easy to miss something when you check the legs the following morning. So I prefer to wait to see what shows up the next day and not mask any potential problems. But any minor cuts will be cleaned with Hibiscrub and have an Animalintex poultice applied.

At a three-day event, I will use a cooling clay as the horse needs all the help he can get to recover for the showjumping next day – and I want to help prevent any overnight swelling which might make him stiffer. I'll ice the legs first to cool them then apply a clay, or I may just soak bandages in iced water, then squeeze the water out and bandage the legs. I redo them later in the evening as they'll have dried and warmed up.

Returning home

When you get home after an event, make a habit of inspecting your horse's legs as soon as you have removed his travel boots and before you put him back in the stable or turn him out in the field. And if you find anything you have missed earlier – for example, a cut under a heel – make sure that you treat it appropriately. I use Forever Living's aloe vera gel for minor grazes.

Small things often respond well to just washing with antiseptic solution and applying a wound cream. If it's a deeper wound, poultice it overnight. Even the most innocent-looking nicks should not be ignored – just in case. Treating a cut instantly could save a hefty vet's bill and a subsequent course of antibiotics because you have noticed it, started treating it early then kept it clean until it healed.

You must be very astute when assessing your horse's legs and you should know them inside and out. If you are familiar with every bump and swelling he usually has, you'll be quick to notice any changes or additional ones that occur.

Check your horse's legs

Trot him up to ensure he's sound

My way

If I get home in daylight, I'll trot up each horse in-hand on a firm, level surface to see if he's stiff. If he's slightly unlevel, I'll trot him up again the following morning to see if he has improved or worsened.

Turn him out

Turnout is very good for horses physically and mentally, so I put mine in the field regularly. This includes the top horses, who will be turned out in pairs. My young horses competing at BE100 or Novice level live in the field all the time so when we get back from an event, I check their legs, put their rugs on, then turn them out. This is good for their mobility because they'll be wandering around all night, which helps to prevent stiffness.

My recovery programme

Next day, bring your horse in from the field or get him out of his stable and run your hands over his legs thoroughly to check again for any signs of swelling, or if there's any extra heat in his feet or legs. Trot him up again in-hand to check that he is sound. However, this is difficult to do on your own, so ask someone to lead him and trot him up while you watch him.

When it comes to time off after a competition, all my horses have a day off after an event. The stabled horses are checked over and trotted up in-hand as a precautionary measure before having rugs and brushing boots on to go out in the field in groups of two or three. Some people think I'm mad turning my horses out in groups and with shoes on, but it works for me. I've always done this because I think that horses are much happier with company.

My horses are usually fed three times a day but when they're turned out after an event, they miss their breakfast feed because they go out first thing. They come in just before lunch to be brushed off and have their feet scrubbed in the wash box, before returning to their stable for a lunchtime feed. Then often they'll lie down for an afternoon nap!

Turnout is good for mobility

A lunchtime feed and then a nap

The horses hack on the third day after an event

For best results

- The second day after an event, my horses spend a total of 50 minutes on the horse walker. They go in both directions (25 minutes each way) and I like them to be marching on in walk. Then they are turned out for a couple of hours.

   The day after that, each horse goes hacking and from then on their workload picks up. They will do their first bit of fast work five days after they have competed, then repeat it every three days ready for their next event.

Kings Temptress

Kings Choice

4 Effective riding

Try not to let the nerves take over as that can affect your riding, turning you from a positive partner to a passive passenger. Your horse needs your support and guidance so effectiveness of the rider is all-important.

2 Understanding and coping with tension

Tension can be caused by a variety of reasons – excitement on the part of the horse, anticipation of the work ahead, nervousness, not trusting the rider. Therefore, find ways of easing the pressure for your horse and helping him to relax – perhaps through lots of steady work, hacks and plenty of turnout. A tense horse will be much happier to be out 24/7 and ideally with a calm companion.

5 Sensitivity

Remember, horses are all very different, so be sensitive to their individual needs. Some require a much more gentle approach, others you can be firmer with – it all depends on their character.

1 Patience and calmness

Be methodical in your teaching. Repetition makes for true understanding. You must be black and white in your training principles as to what is right and what is wrong. Consistently correct mistakes and reward the right response with your voice and/or a pat when your horse produces good work.

3 Thoroughness

Horses like to have a routine so make sure your horse has his – for example, feeding on time and exercise. Make sure that you're organised in your day-to-day running of the yard, that you're on top of paperwork and competition entries, fitness work for you and your horse, and preparation for events.

My keys to success

Riding and competing successfully are all about creating a solid partnership with your horse. And I base mine on 10 tried-and-tested principles...

6 Coping with the lows

Difficult though it may be at the time, try to take a positive out of a negative situation. In eventing, you have to be able to cope with the lows if you want to continue eventing and compete for a long time. And don't let yourself get too low in the lows. Simply work out what went wrong, why it went wrong, how you can make it right and how it could have been prevented. Then enjoy the good times!

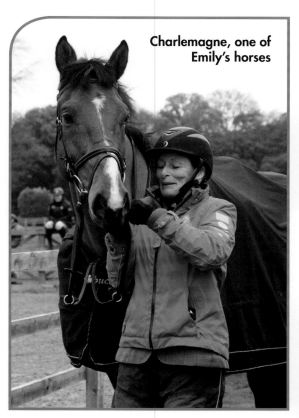

Charlemagne, one of Emily's horses

7 Dedication

Are you prepared to get out there and work, whatever the weather and however you feel?

8 Be open to criticism

As a rider, always be aiming to improve and find a trainer you click with. Even at my age, I realise that I can always learn more. I personally love it when people tell me that I'm not sitting up straight or my reins are too long. I don't take offence, I'm happy for people – especially my trainer Ferdi Eilberg (above) – to point things out that might make a difference.

Imperial Cavalier

9 Positive attitude

Each day, work at being positive in everything you do, especially at events. Try to keep on top of your nerves, don't dwell on the bad points – and smile!

Imperial Cavalier

10 Choosing the right horse

Don't be too proud and persist with a horse who's not living up to your dreams. If a horse you've bought – who you thought would be top class – is not enjoying the work and not performing consistently well for the level of training he's at, be prepared to bite the bullet and sell him on to someone who's less competitive and happy to compete at the lower levels. Keep looking for that right horse – there will be one out there for you.

Acknowledgements

There are many people I would like to thank for their contribution to this book. Firstly my editors, Jane Gazzard and Aimi Clark, designer Paul Smail, plus Roger Trivett of Acanthus Press who – with Peter Appleford and John Bevan – owns my mare Kings Choice and who has taken care of the printing. Many thanks also to Bicton Arena for allowing us to use their wonderful facilities for our photoshoot.

Emily and I could not achieve anything without our hardworking grooms who have worked tirelessly behind the scenes over the years. Of course the support of our owners, past and present, has also been invaluable, particularly Gilly Robinson who took a chance on a young girl with a dream in 1985 and has remained loyal, positive and cheerful throughout the highs and lows that come with the sport.

Finally to the many trainers who have helped me over the years and played a vital role in developing 'my way'. Firstly Sheila Willcox, who helped me form a broad base of knowledge on which to build my career. I also owe thanks to Ferdi Eilberg, Tracie Robinson and Carl Hester for their guidance on the flat, plus Yogi Breisner, Kenneth Clawson, Lars Sederholm, Peter Murphy, Steven Hadley and Pat Burgess in the jumping phases. I dedicate this book to all of you.

With thanks to the following sponsors...

Ariat
Website   www.ariat-europe.com
Tel   01367 242818
Leading performance footwear and apparel for the world's top equestrian athletes

Ascot Buildings
Website   www.ascot-timber.co.uk
Tel   01428 654334
A specialist in equestrian buildings including stables, looseboxes and field shelters

Baileys Horse Feeds
Website   www.baileyshorsefeeds.co.uk
Tel   01371 850247
Family-owned and run horse feed company/ experts in equine nutrition

Bucas
Website   www.bucas.com
Tel   00353 21 431 2200
Supplying highly innovative and technically advanced horse rugs

Clipper Sharp/Smart Grooming
Website   www.clippersharp.com
Tel   01823 681076
Providing clippers, clipper servicing and blade sharpening plus a range of other equine products

Equestrian Rescue Services
Website   www.equinerescue.co.uk
Tel   01300 348997
Nationwide horsebox and trailer roadside assistance and recovery

Forever Living
Website   www.foreverliving.com
Tel   01926 626629
Manufacturers of beneficial wellness products based on aloe vera

Heltor
Website   www.heltor.co.uk
Fuel deliveries, replacement oil tanks, haulage and distribution in Devon and Cornwall

In The Saddle
Website www.inthesaddle.com
Specialists in horse riding holidays around the world

Joules
Website www.joules.com
Tel 0845 250 7170
Clothing for women, men and children plus things for your home and gift ideas

Marksway HorseHage
Website www.horsehageforage.co.uk
Tel 01803 527257
Dust-free forage and the home of the Mollichaff range of high-fibre chaffs and complete feeds

Mitsubishi Motors
Website www.mitsubishi-cars.co.uk
Tel 01285 647774
A car range with something for every equestrian's needs

Mirrors For Training
Website www.mirrorsfortraining.co.uk
Tel 01902 791207
Family-run business supplying made-to-measure training mirrors throughout the UK

Nedz Bed
Website www.nedz.co.uk
Tel 01254 677762
Combining the latest technological advances with the benefits of straw to produce bedding for horses

New Equine Wear
Website www.newequinewear.co.uk
Tel 01172 303700
Protective horse boots, leg wraps, over-reach boots and accessories to fulfil every horse's needs

NFU
Website www.nfu.co.uk
Tel 02476 858500
Offering insurance, pensions and investments, including horse insurance

PolyPads
Website www.polypads.co.uk
Tel 01842 752020
Saddle pads that offer back protection without any saddle fixings. Also leg protectors and pet beds

Point Two Air Jacket
Website www.point-two.co.uk
Tel 01403 732129
A jacket that inflates when you fall off by a lanyard detaching from the saddle

Ride Alert
Website www.alertidgroup.co.uk
Physical identification products for you, your family and horses to wear when riding

Savills
Website www.savills.co.uk
Global real estate services provider listed on the London Stock Exchange

Snuggy Hoods
Website www.snuggyhoods.com
Tel 01225 783399
Protection for your horse whether inside or out – hoods, bibs, sweet-itch rugs and more

StableComfort
Website www.stablecomfort.co.uk
Tel 02870 868463
A shock-absorbing mattress system for stables

SupaStuds
Website www.supastuds.com
Self-cleaning, rust-resistant and specially hardened studs that don't require a tap

Verdon Grey
Website www.verdongrey.co.uk
Tel 01284 812000
Luxury outdoor and all-weather garden furniture

Westgate EFI
Website www.wefi.co.uk
Tel 01303 872277
Meeting all riders' and horses' needs via the Mark Todd, Gatehouse, Coolex ranges

Zoetis
Website www.zoetis.com.uk
Tel 0845 300 8034
Global animal health company

Index